CITYSPOTS
BRUG

Anwer Bati

Written by Anwer Bati

Original photography by Anwer Bati, unless otherwise stated
Front cover photography courtesy of Robert Everts/Getty Images
Series design based on an original concept by Studio 183 Limited

Produced by Cambridge Publishing Management Limited
Project editor: Catherine Burch
Layout: Trevor Double
Maps: PC Graphics
Transport map: © Toerisme Bruges/Johan Mahieu

Published by Thomas Cook Publishing
A division of Thomas Cook Tour Operations Limited
Company Registration No. 1450464 England
PO Box 227, Unit 18, Coningsby Road
Peterborough PE3 8SB, United Kingdom
email: books@thomascook.com
www.thomascookpublishing.com
+ 44 (0) 1733 416477

ISBN-13: 978-1-84157-617-6
ISBN-10: 1-84157-617-4

First edition © 2006 Thomas Cook Publishing
Text © 2006 Thomas Cook Publishing
Maps © 2006 Thomas Cook Publishing
Series Editor: Kelly Anne Pipes
Project Editor: Linda Bass
Production/DTP: Steven Collins

Printed and bound in Spain by GraphyCems

CONTENTS

INTRODUCING BRUGES

Introduction......................................6
When to go 8
The procession of the Holy
    Blood 12
History..14
Lifestyle..16
Culture..18

MAKING THE MOST OF BRUGES

Shopping...22
Eating & drinking 26
Entertainment & nightlife.....30
Sport & relaxation 32
Accommodation 34
The best of Bruges.....................40
Something for nothing 44
When it rains................................46
On arrival.......................................48

THE CITY OF BRUGES

Markt & Burg.............................60
South of Markt 74
Northeast of Markt 90

OUT OF TOWN

Damme 104
Ghent 114
Ypres & World War I
    battlefields............................130

PRACTICAL INFORMATION

Directory.......................................142
Emergencies 156

INDEX...158

MAP LIST

Bruges City 52
Bruges Transport 56
Markt & Burg 61
South of Markt 75
Northeast of Markt...................91
Damme..105
Ghent 115
Ypres...130

SYMBOLS & ABBREVIATIONS

The following symbols are used throughout this book:

ⓐ address   ⓣ telephone   ⓕ fax   ⓔ email   ⓦ website address
ⓛ opening times   ⓝ public transport connections   ⓘ important

The following symbols are used on the maps:

🛈	information office	◯	city
✈	airport	◯	large town
✚	hospital	○	small town
🛡	police station	══	motorway
▤	bus station	▬	main road
▤	railway station	▬	minor road
✝	cathedral	—	railway
❶	numbers denote featured cafés & restaurants		

Hotels and restaurants are graded by approximate price as follows:
£ budget   ££ mid-range   £££ expensive

▶ *This fantastic old mansion is now the Gruuthuse Museum*

INTRODUCING
Bruges

Introduction

It's rather difficult to imagine as you stroll around the streets of Bruges (or Brugge as it is called locally) that, although it is now inland, it was once a major port, and a wealthy trading city – one of the most important in Europe. It is often compared to Venice, not only because of its canals and because of its former importance, but also because its medieval heart is so well preserved. It's sometimes rather crassly called 'The Venice of the North', but it needs no such comparison: it's one of the real gems of Europe in its own right.

The city declined in importance after the 15th century and was a sleepy backwater until it started attracting visitors, many of them British, after the battle of Waterloo. By the end of the 19th century, much of it – particularly its Gothic buildings – had been restored, and tourism became increasingly important. Now Bruges, with a population of 125,000 (only 22,000 of them in the old town) throngs with tourists, both in and out of season, and tourism is its main source of income. A quarter of the foreigners who visit the city are British – easily the largest group.

It's easy to see what the attraction is. It's one of the prettiest cities in Europe, and the local authorities take its appearance very seriously; even today building is strictly controlled and new houses have to use a restricted range of colours, materials and styles. However, the modern is slowly intruding, in the massive shape of the new Concertgebouw (Concert Hall), for instance. Bruges is safe, romantic, and you can easily walk around the centre – often on cobbled streets – or along the canals without much fear of getting lost. It has one of the finest Flemish painting collections in the world, as well as many appealing small museums, and atmospheric churches around every corner. There are plenty of places to eat, drink, shop and stay in – both trendy and traditional – so it's very much a tourist city, a city for couples and families, culture and good living, but it's basically a tranquil place, so don't go expecting a riotous time.

⬤ *Markt is the hub of old Bruges*

When to go

SEASONS & CLIMATE

Belgium's climate is broadly similar to Britain's, but it tends to be colder in winter, and often rainy, foggy or misty, although there isn't usually much snow. Average winter lows are around 1°C (33°F). In summer, the average high is 22°C (72°F), but the temperature can climb into the high 20s (80s).

The main tourist season in Bruges is Easter–September, when it can be swarming with visitors (particularly in the school holidays and in July and August). But it is a year-round city so, if you can, go out of season to avoid the crowds and high season prices in hotels. Spring and autumn are particularly attractive times to visit, and the weather is fairly mild. Winter also has its attractions: most places are open, the shops are emptier, the city is even more welcoming and you can get a hotel room or a table in a decent restaurant without too much trouble. The Christmas Fair in Markt is a good reason to visit at this time. Bruges is perfect for a weekend break or for slightly longer, but remember that the main museums are closed on Monday.

ANNUAL EVENTS

Bruges has major events throughout the year, and increasingly the city is geared to attracting visitors, particularly out of season. Many of the events are outdoors. The leading museums – such as the Groeninge – also mount important special exhibitions from time to time.

March

Cinema Novo Festival A significant film festival at the Cinema Lumière and Ciné Liberty, concentrating on films from Third World countries. ⓦ www.cinemanovo.be

April

Tour of Flanders The first Sunday in April. Major cycle race with around 200 Belgian and international competitors who have to ride over 250 km (155 miles) in a day – starting at Markt Square.
Ⓦ www.rondevanvlaanderen.be

Choco-Laté Chocolate festival, initiated in 2006, and set to expand. At Sint-Janshospitaal, Saaihalle, the Choco-Story Museum and in the city centre. Several of Bruges' best restaurants also offer special menus for chocoholics. Ⓦ www.choco-late.be

🔺 *The canals are the perfect platform for national festivals*

Looking Inside Bruges Antiques and interiors event around town.

May
Melfoor Funfair at 't Zand and Koning Albertpark.

Helig-Bloedprocessie (Procession of the Holy Blood) Ascension Day (17 May in 2007). See page 12 for details.

July
Cactus Festival Usually during the second weekend in July, in Minnewaterpark. A longstanding and buzzy open-air music festival featuring world music, rap, reggae, rock and dance. It sometimes attracts big names. ⓦ www.cactusmusic.be

Belgian National Holiday 21 July. Celebrated with bands and other outdoor entertainment.

Musica Antiqua (Early Music Festival of Flanders) Medieval music concerts from late July to early August, around Bruges city centre in various locations. ⓦ www.musica-antiqua.be

August
Klinkers One of Bruges' liveliest events, and mostly free. A two-week, open-air music and film festival in the city centre which starts at the end of July. The whole town, including restaurants, bars and cafés, gets caught up in the fun. ⓦ www.cactusmusic.be

Lace Days Two days of lace-making demonstrations, stalls and street entertainment.

November
Bruges Festival World Music and folk festival at the Stadsschouwburg (City Theatre) and Biekorf Theatre around the middle of November. It lasts three days, and has been going for almost 20 years.

December
Kerstmarkt (Christmas Market) In Markt, with jolly stalls, mulled wine and a temporary ice rink. It runs daily throughout December, closing at 22.00.

NATIONAL PUBLIC HOLIDAYS
Belgium has a lot of public holidays, and Flanders – where Bruges is – has one all its own, on 11 July. All banks and post offices and public buildings close, as well as many shops, cafés and restaurants. If the holiday falls on a Sunday, places will often be closed on Monday as well. If the holiday is near the end of the week, places may also be closed for the rest of the week.

New Year's Day 1 January
Easter March/April
Labour Day 1 May
Ascension Day (40 days after Easter) May
Whit Monday (Pentecost, seventh Mon after Easter) May/June
Anniversary of the Battle of the Golden Spurs 11 July
Belgian National Holiday 21 July
Feast of the Assumption 15 August
All Saints' Day 1 November
Armistice Day 11 November
Christmas Day 25 December

Procession of the Holy Blood

This constitutes one of the great religious pageants of Europe, of great importance to Bruges, which has a strong Catholic past. It takes place on Ascension Day every year. The mile-long procession – during which the presumed relic of a few dried drops of Christ's blood, and a wooden statue of Christ are paraded – has been held since 1303 in its present form. The relic has attracted pilgrims since 1150 by some accounts, and 1256 by others. The Holy Blood was brought to Bruges in 1149, according to tradition, by Thierry (also known as Derrick or Diederik) of Alsace, Count of Flanders. It is kept in a small crystal and gold phial in Heiligbloed Basiliek (Basilica of the Holy Blood). It was supposedly given to Thierry by his brother-in-law, Baldwin III of Anjou, King of Jerusalem, because of Thierry's heroism during the Second Crusade. However, many historians think that it was acquired during the Fourth Crusade in 1204, after the rapacious sacking of Constantinople.

Whatever the history, now thousands of tourists, as well as the devout, attend the event. Over 1,500 local citizens participate, either dressed in biblical clothes to enact scenes (mostly tableaux on floats) from the Old and New Testaments (including the Last Supper) or wearing medieval costumes for the second part of the ceremony, which celebrates the return of Thierry of Alsace to Bruges. It takes around two and a half hours, starting near the Concertgebouw at 15.00, and ending there. You'll need tickets if you want seats, available from the tourist office at the Concertgebouw, or through the local ticketing and information organisation TINCK (⊙ 070 22 50 05 ⓦ www.tinck.be).

▶ *The phial of 'Holy Blood' has been the centrepiece of the procession since 1303*

History

The earliest recorded mention of Bruges is in the 7th century, as the Municipium Brugense, though there was almost certainly a settlement on the site as early as the 2nd century. The name itself comes from an old Norse word meaning 'jetty' or 'landing place', and appropriately so, because the city – linked to the sea at that time by the Zwin estuary – became a substantial port and trading centre, eventually one of the most important in northwestern Europe.

Bruges was fortified by the counts of Flanders in the 9th century, and reached its commercial pinnacle in the 14th and 15th centuries – particularly in the production of woollen cloth and luxury goods – and traded with countries around Europe and the Mediterranean. In the words of a Spanish visitor in 1437: 'In Bruges, one can find products from England, Germany, Brabant, Holland, Zeeland, Burgundy, Picardy and the major parts of France... I saw oranges and lemons from Castille, as fresh as if they had just been picked, fruit and wine from Greece... I also saw fabrics and spices from Alexandria, and from all corners of the Levant...' Not surprisingly, many foreign merchants were attracted to the city, and some of their trading houses (the equivalent of modern consulates) still stand. Bruges was also the first city to have a formal trading exchange. The house of the local merchants who ran it, the van der Beurse family, exists to this day, and their name ('Bourse') is still used internationally for stock exchanges. Difficult though it is to believe today, at that time ships would moor at Markt Square.

Flanders was ruled by the dukes of Burgundy from the end of the 14th century, and Bruges became an artistic centre, attracting great Flemish painters such as Jan van Eyck and Hans Memling, and fine architecture, as well as growing in stature and power in the region.

Even today, you will find places around town named after Burgundian dukes and duchesses.

But Bruges' fortunes began to suffer by the 16th century, partly because the Zwin estuary silted up so that the city could no longer function as a port, and partly because of the political and religious upheavals of the period. Now under Spanish rule, Bruges was finally cut off from the sea. From then on, it was a story of slow but remorseless decline, and by the end of the 16th century, the city was nicknamed 'Bruges la Morte' (dead Bruges). By the beginning of the 20th century, Bruges was a poor and stagnant medieval town on which the Industrial Revolution had little impact, even though its charms had been rediscovered by visitors since the end of the Napoleonic wars, and much of its architecture had been restored.

The city's life started to improve after the building of the port of Zeebrugge. The cutting of a canal linked Bruges to the sea again in 1907 and slowly, commerce started to revive.

○ *In 2000, Bruges' city centre was designated a UNESCO World Heritage Site*

Lifestyle

Bruges is part of Belgium, of course, but more importantly it is capital of the West Flanders province and very proudly Flemish. Even though Belgium officially has three languages – French, Flemish and German (spoken by a very small minority) – there is now a considerable divide between French speakers (Walloons) and Flemish speakers. In Bruges and the surrounding area, although you will find French on menus, in hotels, and in brochures, programmes and other publications, you won't see it on signs. Only Flemish is used. And Flemish place-names are often not the same as those used by French speakers. So, French Bruges is Flemish Brugge, Ghent is Gent, and Ypres is Ieper. In this book, the place-names most familiar to English-speaking readers are used, with the alternative in brackets.

Flemish is essentially Dutch, and Flemings understand Dutch speakers, though the Dutch sometimes have problems with understanding the Flemish accent. Flemings seem to find English easy to speak, and it is widely spoken, not least because in Flanders many British television programmes are broadcast in English with Dutch subtitles. Some people, and many hotels, also tune in to the main British TV channels. If you speak French, many people will understand it but some will be reluctant to respond. Generally, older and wealthier people still speak French.

Since tourism is the mainstay of Bruges' economy, tourists are cordially received, though over the years there have been some who feel that there are too many tourists. The British appear to be particularly welcome, not only because of the volume of British tourism, but also because of historic links; England provided the wool for local cloth manufacture, and British visitors encouraged the restoration of Bruges in the 19th century. After the British, the main foreign tourists are French, German and Dutch, with smaller numbers of Americans and Japanese.

The residents of Bruges are particularly fond of their city (many never move out), and also of food, drink (particularly beer), music and festivals. The city has a strong Catholic tradition (you'll see small statues of the Virgin Mary on the sides of several houses), perhaps because of the presence of the relic of the Holy Blood in Bruges, but it isn't a particularly religious place today.

⏺ *Refreshment is never far away*

Culture

Bruges was nominated European City of Culture in 2002, and it has a strong artistic tradition going back to the late Middle Ages. Cultural tourism – people wanting to visit Bruges' museums and enjoy its architecture – is central to the city's activities, a fact reflected in the number of local events and festivals.

Most of Bruges' finest medieval buildings, including the Stadhuis (City Hall), were restored in the 19th century, too enthusiastically according to some purists. But they, along with the city's canals, are among the main attractions of the place, whether you actually go in to look at them in detail or simply wander around to soak up the atmosphere.

There are two major museums in Bruges: the Groeninge Museum, with its fine collection of Flemish, Dutch and Belgian paintings and its occasional special exhibitions, and the small Memling Museum in Sint-Janshospitaal (a site to visit in its own right). Other attractive museums are the Arentshuis, which houses a collection of the work of Frank Brangwyn, the 19th/20th-century British artist who was born in Bruges, and the Gruuthuse Museum. And then there are the more idiosyncratic local museums, such as the Museum voor Volkskunde (Folklore Museum) and the Chocolate Museum, not to mention the De Halve Maan Brewery, the last remaining in town. Good value combined tickets entitling you to visit five city museums are sold at the museums and the Concertgebouw. There are concessions for people under 26 and over 60 in the municipal museums (but not private ones). Children under 13 can enter free.

▶ *The Concertgebouw with statues seen from 't Zand Square*

Bruges has more than its fair share of lovely churches and convents, some of which are venues for concerts during Bruges' various music festivals. Joseph Ryelandtzaal is a converted church now used as a classical concert hall. Music is a major feature of the city's life, particularly during the Festival van Vlaanderen (Flanders Festival). The Cactus Festival, Klinkers and the Bruges Festival of World Music offer rather more modern sounds. The Muziekcentrum Cactus (Cactus Music Centre) puts on a diverse range of contemporary music throughout the year (ⓐ Sint-Sebastiaanstraat 4 ⓣ 050 33 20 14 ⓔ info@cactusmusic.be), and several cafés and restaurants around town also offer live music. There is a local symphony orchestra, the Symfonieorkest Vlaanderen.

The main concert hall, or Concertgebouw at 't Zand, one of the few modern buildings in the centre of Bruges, was built to celebrate the 2002 City of Culture accolade. It has its critics, who find it too massive and out of keeping with the local heritage. Others think that its huge auditorium and state-of-the-art features are essential additions to the local cultural scene, and necessary to attract major musical artists, orchestras and opera productions to Bruges.

Cinema is another keen local interest, with the Cinema Novo festival, and the Klinkers festival. The Cinema Lumière shows art-house films, and Ciné Liberty shows more mainstream movies.

The best overall source of information about cultural events in Bruges (and other parts of Flanders) is TINCK, through which you can also book tickets (ⓦ www.tinck.be).

ⓞ *A ride in a horse-drawn carriage is a great way to see the city*

Shopping

One thing Bruges isn't short of is shops of all kinds, from clothing to interior design. Most of them are small and privately run, and many of them are quirky and attractive. There are the usual tacky tourist shops selling souvenirs and 'antiques', of course, and the international chains such as Benetton and Laura Ashley. But you won't find a supermarket or department store in central Bruges, and big-name designer shops are few and far between. However, there are several major Belgian luxury brands represented, such as Delvaux, where a beautifully made handbag will set you back €1,000 or more. For more information on shops, visit www.bruggebusiness.com

WHERE TO SHOP

The main shopping street, with most of Bruges' clothes shops, is Steenstraat, just off Markt, and its continuation, Zuidzandstraat, which leads to 't Zand Square. The area called Zilverpand (between Zuidzandstraat and Noordzandstraat) contains a hotch-potch of little arcades mainly consisting of small boutiques. The other important shopping streets are Geldmuntstraat (a continuation of Noordzandsgtraat), Vlaminstraat (just north of Markt) and Wollestraat, running south of Markt, by the side of Belfort, where you will find the well-known design shop, Callebert. Katelijnestraat and Mariastraat also have numerous shops, but many of them are geared to parting tourists from their money in return for goods of dubious quality and taste. Hoogstraat has a number of antique and interior shops, and St-Amandsstraat is good for jewellery and other luxury goods.

◗ *Herges' famous character lives on in the dedicated Tintin Shop*

WHAT TO BUY

You are unlikely to find any serious bargains in Bruges, but there are many local specialities you might want to take home with you. Chocolates are one of them. Belgian chocolates are famous as among the finest you can buy. There are dozens of shops around town, but some are very much better than others in terms of quality. Chocolaterie Sukerbuyc, Neuhaus and Galler are three of the best. Bruges is famous for its lace, and has been for centuries. There are good lace shops in Wollestraat and Breidelstraat.

There are many good food shops and delicatessens in Bruges, where you can buy the local (or French) cheese, or other specialities

⬤ *Bruges is chocolate heaven for those with a sweet tooth*

such as the wafer-thin biscuits *kletskoppen* (called *dentelles de Bruges*, 'Bruges lace' in French). Try Deldycke delicatessen, where the food is also beautifully displayed.

Wine, cigarettes and cigars are much cheaper in Belgium than they are in Britain, and you'll find plenty of shops selling them. The local drinks are beer and *jenever* (gin), also widely available and easy to take home.

Look out for some of Bruges' quirkier shops such as Teddy & Co, and the Bear Necessities, which sell teddy bears, and the Tintin Shop, where you can buy any number of items based on Hergé's comic-book creation. De Witte Pelikaan sells Christmas decorations year round.

MARKETS

There are morning food markets (08.00–13.00) at Markt (Wed), Beursplein (Sat) and 't Zand Square (Sat), where you will also find cheap clothes on sale. The flea market along Dijver depends on the weather, but it is theoretically open every day in summer (until 18.00) and at weekends during the rest of the year. However, although some things might tickle your fancy, most of what is on sale is hardly worth buying and is firmly aimed at tourists.

USEFUL SHOPPING PHRASES

How much is...?
Hoeveel kost (het)...?
Hoo-fay! kost (het) ...?

Can I try this on?
Mag ik dit passen?
Makh ik dit passen?

I'm a size...
Ik heb maat...
Ik hep maat...

I'll take this one
Deze neem ik
Day-ze naym ik

Eating & drinking

The Belgians are famously fussy about their food, and Flanders is no exception, so it's easy to eat well in almost all price ranges. The food in Flanders has the heartiness and simplicity of Dutch cooking, as well as reflecting the history of the area. So you will find French (particularly Burgundian) dishes on most menus, and even some elements of Spanish cuisine in some local recipes. Menus are normally printed in Flemish and French, and frequently in English as well.

Expect big portions, and prices which might strike you as fairly high – partly because of Belgium's 21 per cent VAT rate. Service is included at a hefty 16 per cent, and there is no need to tip extra (although people sometimes round up the total with small change), unless you have been given particularly special treatment. Prices for set menus are usually lower at lunchtime. If you can, try to avoid Markt and the area immediately around it; you don't have to walk far from here to find somewhere cheaper and better to eat. If you ask for tap water, many restaurants will tell you it isn't safe and will try to sell you mineral water: don't fall for it – the tap water is fine.

Restaurants are generally open for lunch 12.00–14.30 and for dinner 18.00–22.30/23.00 (sometimes later in high season), though some brasseries and cafés serve food throughout the day. Last

RESTAURANT RATINGS
Restaurant ratings in this book are based on the average price of a three-course dinner without drinks. But remember that a one-course lunch or set menu will often be cheaper.
£ Budget under €20   **££** Mid-range €20–75
£££ Most expensive over €75

orders are often by 21.30. Fancier restaurants often close for lunch, frequently on weekends and public holidays. Although there are no big supermarkets in the city centre, there are plenty of small bakeries, stalls, kiosks and delicatessens to buy snacks from for picnics, or you can visit the food markets (see page 25). Canal banks and parks such as Minnewater or Astridpark are great picnic spots.

Many Belgians smoke, but smoking was banned in all enclosed workplaces from the beginning of 2006. It is likely that from 2007, smoking will only be allowed in restaurants in rooms where no hot

UNMISSABLE SPECIALITIES

garnaaltkroketten tasty deep-fried potato croquettes filled with shrimps

hopsheuten hop shoots in cream

maatjes raw herrings

mosselen mussels cooked with white wine, onions and parsley, and eaten with chips

paling in 't groen (*anguilles au vert*) eel cooked in a green sauce of herbs and (normally) spinach

stoemp mashed potatoes mixed with vegetables

vlaamse stoverij (also called *carbonnades Flamandes* and *karbonaden* on menus) a rich and sweet dish of beef stewed in beer, usually served with *frites* (chips)

wafel (*gaufre*) hot waffles, sweet in themselves, but also often served with icing sugar or cream, particularly eaten during festivals and holidays

waterzool chicken or fish broth cooked with cream and vegetables

witloof (*endive* or *chicon*) chicory served in salads or cooked

food is served. Bars and cafés won't be affected. Many places already have non-smoking areas, and some restaurants are smoke-free.

Belgian cuisine is big on meat, particularly steak and chips, with, normally, very good beef. The local fish and seafood (including oysters) are also excellent and widely available, as is high-quality game in season, and charcuterie, but mussels are not of the best quality between April and July. Belgians also seem to have a pronounced sweet tooth so, apart from their famous chocolate,

BELGIAN TIPPLES

You will usually find French wine served in restaurants, but don't forget those other great Belgian tipples – beer and gin. Gin (*jenever* or *genever*) is the favoured spirit in Belgium and is often flavoured, resulting in an aromatic taste distinctly different from British dry gin. It is widely found in bars and in cooking. Beer is taken very seriously in Belgium, and much of it is produced with the same care as goes into wine-making. There are over 600 Belgian beers. Some beers are actually flavoured with fruit and other infusions, and beer is frequently drunk with food and used in cooking. There are many beer bars in Bruges ('t Brugs Beertje, for instance, which serves around 300 types of beer, see page 89). Many beers were originally made in monasteries, and some still are. Among the most famous types of beer are Witbier (a refreshing white beer), Trappist beers (such as Chimay), Lambic (a slightly tangy beer), Geuze (a variation on Lambic, but fizzier and even more sharp), and Kriek (Lambic flavoured with cherries).

ⓘ Beware, some Belgian beers are very strong. Any beer called Tripel is 9 per cent or more in strength.

⬤ *Delicious delicacies are available at the deli counter*

pâtisserie and biscuits are exemplary and delicious. Butter and oil are widely used in cooking, and the excellent local potatoes are a major accompaniment. The ubiquitous *frietjes* (*frites*) are arguably the best chips in the world, not only because of the high quality potatoes found in Belgium, but also because they are fried twice. Thinnish and crisp, they are not only eaten by themselves (often bought from stalls or vans) but served with mussels or accompanied by mayonnaise. In brief, Bruges is not really a place for slimmers, though salads are huge, varied and interesting.

USEFUL DINING PHRASES

I'd like a table for (two) please?
Graag een tafel voor (twee) personen
Khraakh an taa-fel for (tway) persoanen

Could I have the bill please?
De rekening alstublieft?
De ray-ken-ing als-too bleeft?

Waiter!
Ober!
Oaber!

Does it have meat in it?
Zitten er vlees in?
Zitten air vlees in?

Where are the toilets?
Waar is het toilet?
Vaar is het twa-let?

Entertainment & nightlife

Bruges can't really claim to be somewhere to let your hair down or celebrate all night, but the city has just about enough going on in the evening to keep most people happy, particularly after a hard day walking around.

Most restaurants close fairly early, but there are a handful of places which will serve you after 22.00. You can always get a drink

● *The city has many welcoming pubs and bars*

into the early hours, however. Although some shut up shop at fixed times, many bars only close when the last person has left. There are only a few venues where you can dance. There are several bars which play good music (live or recorded), including jazz, blues and contemporary sounds, but frankly, clubbing isn't part of the Bruges scene.

Bruges currently has two cinema complexes, with a third being built outside the city centre. Films are usually shown in their original languages with subtitles. The Lumière, near Markt in a small passageway opposite the Navarra hotel, shows art-house movies on three large screens, with great sound and considerable comfort (@ Sint-Jakobstraat 36 ☎ 050 34 34 65 🌐 www.lumiere.be), and the nearby Cinema Liberty (@ Kuipersstraat 23 ☎ 050 33 2011) shows the latest releases.

Things hot up a little during many of Bruges' festivals, and you will find street entertainment and more venues playing music particularly during the Cactus Festival, Klinkers and the Bruges Festival of World Music. Some restaurants also serve food a little later. You should also check out what's on at the Cactus Music Centre (see page 20), and, for classical music, the Joseph Ryelandtzaal (@ Achiel van Ackerplein, off Ezelstraat ☎ 050 44 86 86). You will find high quality symphonic music and opera at the Concertgebouw, and the occasional dance performance at the Stadsschouwburg (City Theatre), or try to catch a jazz act at the De Werf Arts Centre (@ Werfstraat 108 ☎ 050 33 05 29).

For more information and tickets, contact www.tinck.be (☎ 070 22 50 05) or visit the tourist office (In&Uit Brugge) at the Concertgebouw (☎ 050 44 86 86 🌐 www.brugge.be ◷ 10.00–18.00 Fri–Wed, 10.00–20.00 Thur). Be prepared for long queues in high season.

Sport & relaxation

SPECTATOR SPORTS

Football

There isn't a huge amount of spectator-sport entertainment in Bruges, but the city does have two football teams, Cercle Brugge, and the much more important Club Brugge, a leading Belgian club, with some impressive players, based at the 29,000 capacity Jan Breydel Stadium (outside the centre, to the west). Tickets cost between €20 and €50 depending on the seats. ⓐ Olympialaan 74 ⓣ 050 40 21 35 ⓦ www.clubbrugge.be

Cycling

If you happen to be in Bruges on the first Sunday in April, you can catch the start of the Tour of Flanders at Markt, where thousands gather first thing in the morning to see the cyclists off, in what is the biggest one-day race in cycling.

PARTICIPATION SPORTS

Cycling

Cycling is a fun and popular way to travel about the place, but beware if you're a demon biker; Belgians don't like aggressive bicycling in town, and the streets aren't suitable for it either. You can hire bikes at the railway station (€9.50 for a full day, with your passport and a deposit of €20). There are several other bike-hire places around town, and some hotels also offer the service, often free.

Golf

You can play golf at Damme Golf & Country Club, outside the village of Damme. Greens fees are around €65 during the week or €70 at

the weekend. ⓐ Doornstraat 16 ❶ 050 33 35 72 Ⓦ www.golfinfo.be
🕐 08.30–18.00 (summer); 09.00–17.00 (winter)

Swimming

Some hotels have pools, but if yours doesn't and you want to swim,
there are three main choices: Jan Guilini (ⓐ Keizer Karelstraat 41
Ⓝ Bus: 9 to Visartpark), Interbad (ⓐ Veltemweg 35 Ⓝ Bus: 11 to Sint-
Andreaslyceum) or Olympia (ⓐ Doornstraat 110 Ⓝ Bus: 25 to Jan
Breydel). All of these are outside the city centre.

Walking

Bruges is compact and easy to get around by foot, so most people
get a lot of walking in their visit to this charming city. If you want to
get the heart pumping a little harder, you can walk to Damme, or
climb the 366 steps to the top of Belfort. No matter where you
wander, you can always find rest for tired feet by letting a horse or a
boat take the strain for you – carriage rides go from Markt Square
and canal trips are widely available.

⬥ There's no better way to relax and sightsee than on a canal trip

Accommodation

Bruges might not be a big place, but it certainly punches above its weight in terms of the number and types of hotels (over 100), and other accommodation on offer. Even some of the cheaper hotels are on canals or housed in lovely old buildings. There are plenty of up-market hotels around if you want to splash out on a romantic weekend. Many hotels include a buffet breakfast in their rates, others charge a hefty supplement. It's generally sensible to book well in advance, particularly in the main season; turning up and hoping for the best is risky. Tour operators and Eurostar offer some of the best inclusive deals.

As a general rule, the nearer a hotel is to Markt, the more expensive it will be. There is little point in staying outside the centre of Bruges unless you are on a very tight budget, particularly if you are visiting for a short time; travel in and out of town will limit what you can see, and could prove costly if you have to take a taxi back to your hotel in the evening.

HOTELS
Unless you have booked an inclusive package, it pays to investigate your options thoroughly on the web. The Bruges tourist website

---

ACCOMMODATION RATINGS

Accommodation ratings are based on the average price of a double room per night, including breakfast:

£ Budget	under €140
££ Mid-range	€140 to €200
£££ Most expensive	over €200

(www.brugge.be) carries a comprehensive list of hotels, their facilities and locations. It also provides links to the hotels' own websites. The website also lists several self-catering apartments which are a good choice if you want to stay for more than a few days.

You are likely to get good deals in spring, autumn and winter, and during the week. Weekends and high season will usually be more expensive. Listed below are a few recommendations, but there are many more good hotels to choose from.

Adornes £ On St Anna Canal in a group of 16th- and 18th-century houses. Not in the main tourist area, but only a 15-minute walk away from Markt. Free bicycles for guests. ⓐ Sint-Annarei 26 ⓣ 050 34 13 36 ⓦ www.adornes.be

🔺 *Hotels overlooking the canal can be pricier than others*

Botaniek £ A small, quiet hotel in an 18th-century house. Well-situated between Astrid Park and the Dijver. ⓐ Waalsestraat 23 ⓣ 050 34 14 24 ⓦ www.botaniek.be

Ter Brughe £ In a 16th-century house on a canal north of Markt. It's worth going for one of the more expensive rooms.
ⓐ Oost-Gistelhof 2 ⓣ 050 34 03 24
ⓦ www.hotelterbrughe.com

● *Traditionally decorated rooms at De Tuilerieen*

Ter Duinen £ Some way north of Markt, but on a canal. Well-run and friendly, with double-glazed rooms. ⓐ Langerei 52 ⓣ 050 33 04 37 ⓦ www.terduinenhotel.be

Martin's Brugge ££ A modern hotel, trendily decorated, with a good bar and comfortable rooms, near Markt. ⓐ Oude Burg 5 ⓣ 050 44 51 11 ⓦ www.martins-hotel.com

Montanus ££ An unusual hotel, not far from the Begijnhof and the Church of Our Lady. There are some chalet-type rooms in the large garden, as well as more conventional rooms in the main building. All are comfortable. ⓐ Nieuwe Gentweg 78 ⓣ 050 33 11 76 ⓦ www.montanus.be

Oud Huis de Peelaert ££ In an imposing old mansion, close to Burg and the St Anna district, this is a good central base, with old-fashioned but well-decorated and spacious rooms. ⓐ Hoogstraat 20 ⓣ 050 33 78 89 ⓦ www.depeelaert.com

Crowne Plaza ££–£££ It would be difficult to be more central than this modern hotel (with a pool and many other facilities) on the Burg. ⓐ Burg 10 ⓣ 050 44 68 44 ⓦ www.crowneplaza.com/bruggebel

Pandhotel ££–£££ Exceptionally stylish boutique hotel, with beautifully decorated rooms and a cosy lounge and bar. Very well located for Bruges' main attractions. Family-run (mother and daughter) and friendly. ⓐ Pandreitje 16 ⓣ 050 34 06 66 ⓦ www.pandhotel.com

De Tuilerieen £££ One of Bruges' most prestigious old-style hotels, where many celebrities have stayed. Service is friendly, however, and the rooms particularly attractive, especially those overlooking the Dijver Canal. Even the new rooms are decorated in a traditional way. It is very close to many of the city's main sights, and has a small swimming pool. ⓐ Dijver 7 ⓣ 050 34 36 91 ⓦ www.hoteltuilerieen.com

Relais Ravenstein £££ Opened in 2004, this is one of Bruges' most modern hotels, with contemporary décor, large rooms, state-of-the-art facilities, a very good restaurant and a welcoming bar. The hotel has a canal terrace where you can eat or drink. ⓐ Molenmeers 11 ⓣ 050 47 69 47 ⓦ www.relaisravenstein.be

BED & BREAKFAST

Bruges has many bed-and-breakfast establishments, some of them very stylish indeed, others more modest. Prices range from around €60 per night for a double room to over €150. Among the most luxurious are:

Huyze Hertsberge ££ Centrally located, with a garden next to a canal. ⓐ Hertsbergestraat 8 ⓣ 050 33 35 42 ⓦ www.huyzehertsberge.be

Huyze die Maene ££ Actually in Markt Square, in one of the square's oldest buildings, above one of Bruges' better brasseries. ⓐ Markt 17 ⓣ 050 33 39 59 ⓦ www.huyzediemaene.be

YOUTH HOSTELS

Bruges has a number of youth hostels, of varying degrees of comfort and cleanliness. They all charge around €15–18 per person per night if you share a room or dormitory, more if you want a room to yourself.

Bauhaus International Youth Hostel £ To the east of Markt, but not too far away, and has a restaurant. ⓐ Langestraat 135–137 ⓣ 050 34 10 93 ⓦ www.bauhaus.be ⓝ Bus: 6 & 16

Charlie Rockets £ Very central, and lively with snooker and a bar. ⓐ Hoogstraat 19 ⓣ 050 33 06 60 ⓦ www.charlierockets.com

International Youth Hostel Europa £ An official hostel in a southern suburb, in its own grounds. ⓐ Baron Ruzettelaan 143 ⓣ 050 35 26 79 ⓦ www.vjh.be ⓝ Bus: 2 & 749

Passage £ One of the best choices, it's close to St Saviour's Cathedral and all the main attractions, and has a bar. ⓐ Dweerstraat 26 ⓣ 050 34 02 32 ⓦ www.passagebruges.com

Snuffel Backpacker Hostel £ To the northwest of Markt. Relaxed, with a bar and bikes for rent. ⓐ Ezelstraat 47–49 ⓣ 050 33 31 33 ⓦ www.snuffel.be ⓝ Bus: 3 & 13

CAMPSITES

There is only one campsite in Bruges, beyond the outer canal of the city centre, to the east. Camping Memling ⓐ Veltemweg 109 ⓣ 050 35 58 45 ⓦ www.campingmemling.be ⓝ Bus: 11

THE BEST OF BRUGES

Since central Bruges is so compact, you can easily see most of the main sights in a weekend. Just wandering around can be as rewarding as visiting museums and churches, or you can take walking, cycling, horse-drawn carriage and canal tours around town.

TOP 10 ATTRACTIONS

- **Markt and Belfort** You will inevitably pass or go through Markt many times if you walk around. The market square and bell tower are the hub of old Bruges (see pages 60–62 & 63).

- **Groeninge Museum** Bruges' main museum, with a splendid collection of Flemish art (see pages 79–80).

- **Sint-Janshospitaal and Memling Museum** The medieval hospital complex is not only attractive in itself, but also houses an excellent gallery (see pages 82–3).

- **Burg** Next to Markt, this square houses the Basilica of the Holy Blood, the 12th-century church where the supposed relic of the blood of Christ is kept. The grand City Hall occupies another side of the square (see page 63).

- **Begijnhof (Beguinage)** The garden and historic houses are a beautiful and peaceful place to wander around (see pages 76–7).

- **Gruuthuse Museum** The huge mansion of the Lords of Gruuthuse dates from when Bruges was at its commercial zenith (see page 81).

- **Onze-Lieve-Vrouwekerk (Church of Our Lady)** This vast medieval church, with its 122-m (400-ft) high spire, is one of the city's main landmarks (see pages 81–2).

- **Canal walk** Taking a walk around any of Bruges' canals will lead you past numerous lovely houses and other sights, and offers good picnic spots.

- **Canal-boat trip** A great way to see Bruges and get a feel for the place (see page 58).

- **Horse-drawn carriage ride** Touristy? Well yes, but the ride takes you past many of Bruges' main attractions (see page 58).

◗ *A great way to see Bruges is on a canal trip*

Your at-a-glance guide to seeing and experiencing the best of Bruges, depending on the time you have available.

HALF-DAY: BRUGES IN A HURRY

Half a day isn't really enough to do justice to the city, but it will tempt you to come back. Walk around Markt and Burg, then visit the Groeninge Museum, the Gruuthuse Museum and, if you have time, the Church of Our Lady. They are all very near one another. If that seems too museum-heavy for you, simply take a canal trip from outside Sint-Janshospitaal, or a horse-drawn carriage trip around town from Markt, and pop into the Groeninge Museum, even if just for a short time.

1 DAY: TIME TO SEE A LITTLE MORE

If you have a whole day in Bruges, as well as the above, go to Sint-Janshospitaal and the Memling Museum, take a walk along any of the canals, visit the Begijnhof, and perhaps the nearby De Halve Maan Brewery. Try to have lunch away from Markt, or be prepared to suffer the high prices. If you want to go shopping, Steenstraat is your best bet.

2–3 DAYS: SHORT CITY BREAK

You can see most of Bruges' main attractions in three days, in a reasonably relaxed way. You'll have time to actually go inside the Heiligbloed Basiliek (Basilica of the Holy Blood), the Stadhuis (City Hall), and Sint-Salvatorskathedraal (St Saviour's Cathedral), and see its treasury and collection of paintings. The Concertgebouw is near the cathedral and might well have a special exhibition on; the building affords great views from the roof. You could also try to walk to the top of Belfort and be rewarded by even better views of the city. You should definitely take a boat trip on the canals, spend longer in the Onze-

Lieve-Vrouwekerk (Church of Our Lady) and its museum, visit the peaceful pharmacy at Sint-Janshospitaal, and the fun Archaeology Museum in the same complex. Choco-Story, the enticing chocolate museum, is also well worth a visit. If you feel like a quiet walk, try the pretty St-Anna district, where you'll find the Folklore Museum, the English convent, the Lace Centre, and several charming churches. But remember that museums and most churches close at 17.00.

LONGER: ENJOYING BRUGES TO THE FULL

Now you really can relax, and linger over a long lunch or two, or indulge yourself in the shops. You can go inside the Arentshuis (Brangwyn Museum), visit the windmills and city gates on Bruges' outer canal, and maybe take in the Diamant Museum (Diamond Museum). You could also go to the Guido Gezelle Museum, dedicated to one of Flanders' best-known poets, and the museum of Our Lady of the Pottery. Consider visiting the lovely nearby village of Damme, the city of Ghent (which has almost as many attractions as Bruges), or Ypres and the World War I battlefields (see 'Out of Town').

● *The Groeninge Museum's collection of Flemish art spans 600 years*

Something for nothing

Bruges isn't a cheap place. However, there are many things you can do that won't cost you a cent. The most enjoyable is probably simply walking around town and taking in the architecture. Among the lovely old houses and public buildings (many much more recent than they seem, thanks to the local building policy and the

⬤ *No price can be put upon the sheer beauty of Bruges' ancient architecture*

extensive restoration that has taken place in Bruges over the last century or more), you'll also notice the occasional extremely modern house, as compatible contemporary architecture is given special exemption from building restrictions.

Bruges' many churches (but not its museums) are also free, and even the smallest are worth visiting, but don't miss out on the three most important: the Heiligbloed Basiliek (Basilica of the Holy Blood), the Onze-Lieve-Vrouwekerk (Church of Our Lady), and Sint-Salvatorskathedraal (St Saviour's Cathedral). The Begijnhof (but, again, not the museum) is also free to enter.

Likewise, the Sint-Janshospitaal enclave or the grounds of the Arenthuis Museum are all free to walk around and admire from the outside. The same is true of the Concertgebouw, impressive if you like modern architecture.

Bruges has many charming squares to sit in, such as Jan van Eycksplein. Some are very small, but many of them have benches and small cafés so you can sit back and contemplate life. If you stay away from the area around Markt, and the so-called 'golden triangle' (an area bordered by the streets just north of Markt, 't Zand Square, the Dijver and the Begijnhof) where prices are high, keeping yourself watered and fed needn't burn a hole in your wallet.

Then there are the small parks, Minnewaterpark and Astridpark, where you can relax without paying a penny. Astridpark has a small pond and a colourful bandstand, and the romantic Minnewater Park is built on a lake ('the Lake of Love').

If you go to Bruges during one of its festivals, particularly in the summer, you'll find free entertainment in the streets. Window-shopping won't cost you anything, unless you want to give in to temptation of course; and the same may be said for wandering around the markets at Markt or 't Zand.

When it rains

It rains quite a lot in Bruges, so make sure you take an umbrella or something waterproof, even in summer. However, if you're unlucky enough to be there when it really pours, you will be able to pass many happy hours in the Groeninge Museum. If you decide to take refuge in a bar or café, why not try some of the local beer – and then you can go and find out how it was made by taking a tour around the De Halve Maan Brewery. Or, if you're in the mood for something sweeter, Choco-Story, the chocolate museum, will delightfully tickle your taste-buds. Light relief from such waist-widening pleasures is to be found in the Lace Centre in the Jerusalem Church, or in the Diamond Museum, where you'll see how the precious stuff is cut.

Lace-making and diamond-cutting can make you thirsty, so treat yourself to a drink in one of the grander hotels, whose prices – surprisingly – are on a par with the majority of bars in the main tourist area. Once suitably revived, you can look around their public areas.

The horse-drawn carriages are covered, so, even if the poor horses get soaked, you can safely take a ride in the rain. Many people – properly wrapped – think nothing of taking a canal boat in bad weather, or even walking along the canals. Then there's always shopping, although most shops are small and don't take much time to get around.

Otherwise, you can go and see a movie at the arty Lumière cinema, or the more mainstream Ciné Liberty. Alternatively, just have a long lunch and enjoy Flanders culture on a more gastronomical level.

▶ *The splendid interior of St-Walburgakerk is worth seeing – come rain or shine*

On arrival

TIME DIFFERENCES

Belgium is on Central European Time (GMT + 1 hour). During Daylight Saving Time (late Mar–late Sept), the clocks are put ahead one hour. At 12.00 in Bruges in the middle of summer, times elsewhere are as follows:

Australia Eastern Standard Time 20.00, Central Standard Time 19.30, Western Standard Time 18.00
New Zealand 22.00
South Africa 12.00
UK 11.00
USA and **Canada** Newfoundland Time 07.30, Atlantic Canada Time 07.00, Eastern Time 06.00, Central Time 05.00, Mountain Time 04.00, Pacific Time 03.00, Alaska 02.00

ARRIVING

By air

The nearest international airport to Bruges is **Brussels Airport**, 14 km (9 miles) outside Brussels. It is easy to get into the capital, and from there it is possible to get a train connection to Bruges from either the Gare du Midi/Zuid or Gare Centrale/Centraal. You can take a train, the Airport City Express, which takes around 25 minutes and costs a few euros. There are three or four trains an hour. There is a bus, the Airport Line (No. 12), which runs approximately every 20 minutes and takes 35 minutes to get in to central Brussels. Taxis to town are naturally more expensive, and cost €30–40. Buses and taxis leave from level 0 of the airport, and trains from level 1. There are car-rental offices in the arrivals hall, where you will also find a bank, a bureau de change and an information desk. For more information visit www.brusselsairport.be

Ryanair operates low cost flights to **Charleroi Airport**, about an hour's drive from Brussels. Charleroi town has two stations (Ouest and Sud), and you can take a bus to either of them from the airport, and then get a train to Brussels, around 50 minutes away, leaving every half hour or so. Charleroi Sud is the best choice, with a total travel time to Bruges of about 2 hours. You can also take a shuttle bus from Charleroi Airport directly to Brussels. It stops near the Gare du Midi/Zuid. If you decide to take the shuttle back to Charleroi, beware that some rogue taxi drivers might tell you that the service

◆ *For a day trip to nearby Damme, maybe go by barge?*

isn't working, in order to persuade you to use them instead. Taxis in to Brussels can cost up to €100, but you can arrange a private transfer (see www.ryanair.com) from €15 per person.

By rail

If you travel by Eurostar, the train terminates in Brussels at the Gare du Midi/Zuid. Trains to Bruges go from the same station, and you

● Bruges at night is a beautiful and safe place to wander around

can use your Eurostar ticket for them, at no extra cost. The journey takes some 55 minutes on a local train. Apart from the destination board, it is very difficult to get train information at the station, so it is advisable to check timetables before you leave home at www.b-rail.be

🛈 Beware of pickpockets at the station, particularly if you are in one of the shops, bars or cafés.

Bruges Station, at Stationsplein, is a 10–15 minute drive or bus journey from the centre. You can also walk to the centre in about 20 minutes. There is a café and a tourist information point. The No. 12 bus goes from the station to 't Zand and Markt from 07.48 to 18.31 on weekdays, and 09.11–18.51 at weekends. At the time of writing, it costs just €1. There is also a taxi rank at the station.

By coach
Buses and coaches stop at the bus station next to Bruges Station at Stationsplein.

By car
Bruges is surrounded by a ring road, from which there are several routes to the centre, but it isn't a particularly car-friendly city; there are tricky one-way systems in the centre which only local experts can easily navigate, and limited parking. There are car parks at 't Zand, Biekorf, Begijnhof, Pandretie and at the station, but they fill up fast, particularly in the summer. The station is the best and cheapest parking option, operating 7 days a week, and costing €0.50 an hour. The maximum for 24 hours at the station is €2.50. Street parking in the main streets of the centre is metered from 09.00 to 19.00, and you

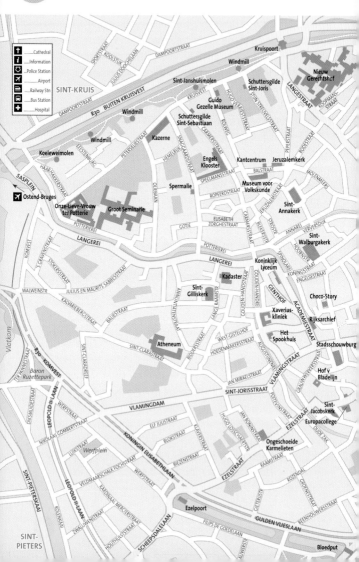

Bruges City

0 — 250 metres
0 — 250 yards

can't park for more than two hours. There are also 'blue zones' (09.00–19.00) in Bruges, where you can park for up to four hours if you display a blue parking disc (which you can buy from garages and tobacconists). Blue-zone restrictions are lifted on Sundays and Belgian public holidays. Watch out, too, for resident-only parking areas.

FINDING YOUR FEET

Bruges is a relaxed and friendly place, but one that expects that visitors are there for the culture and cuisine and assumes they will be well behaved and fairly conventionally dressed. Casual clothes are fine, though you might want to dress up if you plan to go to a fancy restaurant or stay in one of the top hotels. Although it is safe to walk around, the city attracts its fair share of pickpockets, like any major tourist destination, particularly in the summer, so take care with handbags and wallets. Since many of the locals speak English and are very helpful, you should easily be able to find your way around. It is difficult to get very lost in central Bruges in any case. Don't forget to pack comfortable walking shoes, as you will be walking most of the time. Because many of the medieval streets are

IF YOU GET LOST, TRY …

Do you speak English?
Spreekt u Engels?
Spraykt-oo Eng-els?

Is this the way to…?
Is dit de weg naar…?
Is dit de vekh naar…?

Could you point it out on the map?
Kunt u het op de kaart aanwijzen?
Kunt oo het op de kaart aan-wayezen?

small and one-way, the pace of the traffic is slow, so it's generally safe to cross the road anywhere, although UK visitors should remember that the traffic will come from the left, not the right, and bicycles are allowed to go the wrong way down one-way streets.

ORIENTATION

Central Bruges is a small place, and once you've found Markt, Burg and the Belfort (the belfry of the market hall in Markt), it should be relatively easy to find your way around, not least because you can see the Belfort from much of Bruges. The spires of the Church of Our Lady and St Saviour's Cathedral and the huge new terracotta-coloured Concertgebouw at 't Zand are other good landmarks.

GETTING AROUND

The centre of Bruges (the only place you will want to go in town) is only 3 km (17/8 miles) across and in an oval, surrounded by the

🔺 *The Lace Days festival is in August*

KOOLKERKE
SINT-KRUIS
SINT-JOZEF
HAVEN
SINT-PIETERS
CHRISTUS-KONING
SINT-ANDRIES
7 Dampoort
6 Kruispoort
8 Ezelpoort
1 Bloedput
P&R Boogschutterslaan
± 0,7 km
P RAND
RING
ZONE 1 CENTRUM
LANGEREI
VLAMINGDAM
ST.-JORISSTRAAT
EZELSTRAAT
SPANJAARDSTR.
AKADEMIESTR.
VLAMINGSTRAAT
SPIEGELREI
LANGESTRAAT
ST.-JAKOBSTR.
HOF SEBRECHTS
GRAAF VISART PARK
E40 Veurne - Gent - Brussel
A10 Oostende
E403 A17 Kortrijk - Roeselare
N31 Zeebrugge

Key

TAXI taxi stands

motorcycle / scooter bay

bike rental

main city roads

metered parking

bus stop

P500 central car park with free shuttle bus

peripheral car park on the ring

ZONE 1 CENTRUM
from 9 am until 7 pm
max. parking duration: 4h

ZONE 2 WEST-BRUGGE
from 9 am until 7 pm
max. parking duration: 4h
No parking in residents' parking areas

P TICKET € MAX 2 U/H

ZONE P Centrum-stad Centrum-ville Zentrum City centre MAX 4 U/H

P&R Steenbrugge ± 2 km

P&R Jan Breydel ± 2,5 km

P RAND + gratis bus

ZONE 30 km in de binnenstad
in the entire city centre

P500 Centrum Station + gratis bus

P433

ASSEBROEK

BURG

SINT-MICHIELS

ZONE 1 CENTRUM

ZONE 2 WEST-BRUGGE

5 Gentpoort

4 Katelijnepoort

3 Boeveriepoort

2 Smedenpoort

RING

KING

STATION

outermost canal. So it shouldn't take more than 45 minutes, at a leisurely pace, to cross from one end to another. As a result, and because of the traffic problems mentioned above, walking or cycling are always the best options. Although cyclists are allowed to go in both directions in one-way streets, they aren't allowed in pedestrian-only areas.

The local bus service is good, but only really necessary for going to the railway station. The only two taxi ranks are at Markt and the railway station. You can't hail one on the street, but your hotel or restaurant will call you one. They aren't cheap, and you will be expected to tip 10–15 per cent. The Bruges visitors' guide lists the local taxi companies.

Other ways of seeing the city include canal tours (30 minutes, 10.00–18.00 Mar–Nov, €5.70 for adults), for which there are a number of starting points, mini-coaches (50 minutes) leaving from Markt Square, and horse-drawn carriages starting at Markt and ending at Begijnhof (30 minutes, €30 per four- or five-person carriage).

You can also take a guided mini-coach trip to Damme, and return on a canal barge, with a bus then taking you to Markt. Or you can take the barge both ways. Trains from the local station go to Ghent (Gent) or Ypres (Ieper), though you will have to change at Kortrijk for the latter (see 'Out of Town' for more details).

CAR HIRE

It's really only worth hiring a car if you want to travel outside Bruges. All the major companies, as well as local ones, are represented. But it's best to book before you arrive, particularly in high season. Otherwise, your hotel will normally be able to help you.

◉ *There are breathtaking views of the city from the Concertgebouw*

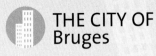

THE CITY OF
Bruges

Markt & Burg

The market square, Markt, and the adjoining Burg Square, are the hub of old Bruges. You will pass through Markt – with its cafés and the shopping streets around it – several times, even on the shortest visit. And the old market hall, with its towering belfry (Belfort), is the most important landmark in town. The smaller and much less busy Burg was the original heart of Bruges.

SIGHTS & ATTRACTIONS

Markt

Despite the high prices, you will inevitably want to have a drink or a coffee, at least, in one of Markt's many cafés, simply to feel part of what Bruges is all about, and to people-watch. You might also want to take a horse-drawn carriage ride or a guided minibus tour starting from there.

If you're feeling fit, you can walk to the top of the **Belfort** (belfry, 366 spiral steps) and get some great views of Bruges and the countryside around it. Be warned that it's a long way up (and down), and it can get very windy at the top (although the viewing area is enclosed). The 19th-century statue in the centre of the square commemorates Pieter de Coninck and Jan Breydel, who led a rebellion against the French in the early 14th century, resulting in the massacre of several thousand Frenchmen.

Most of the buildings in Markt are reconstructions. On the west side of the square is the **Craenenburg** café, which looks ancient but was rebuilt in the 1950s. Dominating the east side of the square is the neo-Gothic **Provinciaal Hof**, the regional government building for West Flanders (of which Bruges is the capital). It was built in the

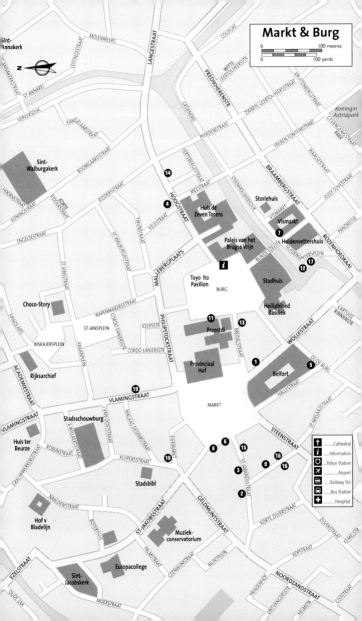

Markt & Burg

| 0 | | | | 100 metres |
| 0 | | | | 100 yards |

Sint-Annakerk

MOLENMEERS
LANGESTRAAT
COUPURE
PREDIKHERENSTR
WITTE LEERTOUWERSSTR
CROENERE!
PEERDENSTRAAT
PREDIKHERENSTR
ZWARTE LEERTOUWERSSTR
FREREN FONTEINSTRAAT
KRUITENBERGSTRAAT
BRAAMBERGSTRAAT
JOZEF SUYVESTRAAT
C. VAN CAUSTRAAT
G-VAN-OOSTSTRAAT
KONINGIN ASTRIDPARK

ST ANNAREI
VERVERSDIJK
KANOE LAARSTRAAT

ST JANSSTRAAT

Sint-Walburgakerk

"MOORSTRAAT
KONINGSTRAAT
KORTE RIDDERSTR
RIDDERSTRAAT
BOOMGAARDSTRAAT
BIDDERSTRAAT
KELKSTRAAT
TWINSTRAAT
ST WALBURGASTRAAT
HOOISTRAAT
KEERSBERGSTRAAT
MEESTRAAT
STEENHOUWERSDIJK
VISMARKT
ROZENHOEDKAAI
PANDREITJE
HUIDENVETTERSSTR

14

Storiehuis

Huis de Zeven Torens

Vismarkt ⑦

Huidenvettershuis ⑫ ⑰

Paleis van het Brugse Vrije

ℹ

Toyo Ito Pavilion

BURG

BLINDE EZELSTR
HUIDENVETTERSPLEIN

Stadhuis

Heiligbloed Basiliek

WOLLESTRAAT
OUDE BURG
KARTUIZE RINNENSER

Choco-Story

ENGELSESTRAAT
ST JANSSTRAAT
SPINOLAREI
WAPENMAKERSSTRAAT
CORDO EANIERSSTR
KRANNELEN
KEERSSTR
CORDO EANIERSSTR
PHILIPSTOCKSTRAAT

ST-JANSPLEIN

BISKAJERSPLEIN

Rijksarchief

⑲ **Proostdi** ⑪ ⑬

BREIDELSTRAAT

Provinciaal Hof

① ⑤

Belfort

HALLESTRAAT

MARKT

ACADEMIESTRAAT
VLAMINGSTRAAT
A MILAERTSTRAAT
ROBIINSTRAAT
GRAUWWERKERSSTRAAT
NAALOENSTRAAT

Stadsschouwburg

Huis ter Beurze

VLAMINGSTRAAT

ST-NIKLAASSTRAAT
STEENSTRAAT
KORTE ZILVERSTRAAT
ZILVERSTR

⑧ ⑥ ⑮ ⑱

J VAN OOSTSTRAAT
NIKLAAS DESPARSTRAAT
KUIPERSSTRAAT
EIERMARKT

⑩ ⑨ ⑯

③

Stadsbibl ②

Hof v Bladelijn

Sint-Jacobskerk

BOTERHUIS
ST-JAKOBSSTRAAT
PALMSTRAAT
GELDMUNTSTRAAT
GEENMUNTSTRAAT
MUNTPLEIN
PRINSENHOF
ONTVANGERSTR
KOPSTRAAT
NOORDZANDSTRAAT
HELMSTR

Muziek-conservatorium

Europacollege

EZELSTRAAT
OUDE ZAK
MOERSTRAAT

†	......Cathedral
ℹ	......Information
	......Police Station
✈	......Airport
🚉	......Railway Stn
🚌	......Bus Station
✚	......Hospital

late 19th century, after a neoclassical building on the same site was destroyed by fire. You can see a painting of the earlier building in the Groeninge Museum. Even earlier, the late 13th-century Waterhalle – a covered hall over a canal, where goods were unloaded from barges – was located on the site. It was pulled down in 1789.

There is a **market** here on Wednesday mornings, and the square is also the scene of Bruges' famous Christmas market.

◔ *The Belfort towers above Markt*

Burg

The Burg, from which Bruges grew outwards, contains several important and highly decorated buildings (see 'Culture'). In a startling contrast, on the site of a demolished church, you will see the **Toyo Ito Pavilion**, designed by innovative Japanese architect Toyo Ito to celebrate Bruges' selection as European City of Culture in 2002. The 22-m (72-ft) long pavilion is made of glass and honeycombed aluminium, and is surrounded by a small, circular pond. It's a good place to have a rest or to escape the rain. Just off the Burg is the **Vismarkt** (fish market), where fish is sold on stone slabs in the mornings Tues–Sat. The section of canal called **Gronerei**, near the Burg, is one of the prettiest in Bruges, and is regularly featured on postcards.

CULTURE

Belfort (belfry)

The old market halls behind the Belfort in Markt now contain an art gallery and public loos. Inside the belfry itself, which is floodlit at night, you will find a souvenir shop. The 83-m (272-ft) high tower came to symbolise Bruges' importance when it was at its wealthiest. The oldest part (nearest the ground) dates from the 13th century; the bell tower was added 200 years later. The Belfort belongs to the Bruggemuseum, a collective name for the six most important historic sites in Bruges. If you decide to climb up, you will pass the treasury, the clock mechanism, and finally a mechanism that controls the carillon of 47 bells which chime every quarter-hour. There can be long queues for the climb, so get there early.

ⓐ Markt 7 ⓦ www.brugge.be ⓒ 09.30–17.00, last admission 16.15, closed Mon; admission charge

Heiligbloed Basiliek (Basilica of the Holy Blood)

In a corner of Burg Square, small and easy to miss, with an ornately decorated façade, the church has two chapels: St Basil's Chapel on the ground floor (built 1139–49), with its austere medieval Romanesque style, and, rebuilt in the 19th century, the neo-Gothic chapel upstairs where the relic of the Holy Blood is kept with other religious objects and some paintings in a small treasury.

ⓐ Burg 15 ⓦ www.brugge.be ⓛ 09.30–12.00 & 14.00–18.00 (summer); 10.00–12.00 & 14.00–16.00, closed Wed (winter); small admission charge for treasury

Paleis van het Brugse Vrije (Palace of the Liberty of Bruges)

Built in 1525, this was originally the administrative centre for the semi-autonomous area of Bruges Liberty in the Middle Ages – run by 4 burgomasters and 24 aldermen – until the French put an end to local rule during the Revolution. After that it became the city's courthouse until the 1980s. The façade you will see in the square dates from the early 18th century, though the exterior of the building facing the neighbouring canal is original.

It's not a must-see, but inside the Renaissance Chamber, once the meeting place for the aldermen, you will find a huge fireplace made of oak, alabaster and marble, designed in the 16th century by the master craftsman Lanceloot Blondel. The building now houses Bruges' archives. It is part of the Bruggemuseum group that consists of the six most significant historic sites in Bruges. Your palace ticket (€2.50) will also gain you entry to the Stadhuis and vice versa. It includes an audioguide.

ⓐ Burg 11a ⓦ www.brugge.be ⓛ 09.30–12.30 & 13.30–17.00, closed Mon

---

ⓞ *The façade of the Heiligbloed Basiliek is intricately decorated*

· M · V · XXIII ·

Stadhuis (City Hall)

Next to the palace, Bruges' grand City Hall dates from 1376 and is the oldest in Flanders, hence its status as one of the six top historical sites in Bruges. It has been restored on several occasions so that the only reliably medieval part left today is the vaulted wooden ceiling of the Gothic Hall on the first floor, erected in 1385. The paintings on the walls of this vast council chamber depict the history of Bruges and date from the 19th century. The room next door houses a collection of artefacts, maps and other illustrations of the city's history. There are further exhibits – including paintings – on the ground floor. An audioguide is included in the entry charge, which also gives you access to the Paleis van het Brugse Vrije (see page 64).

ⓐ Burg 12 ⓦ www.brugge.be ⓛ 09.30–17.00, closed Mon

RETAIL THERAPY

Most of Bruges' best shops are in the streets off Markt – Steenstraat, Wollestraat and Geldmuntstraat. Steenstraat, coming off the west of Markt, and the area around it, houses most of Bruges' top clothes shops and several chocolate shops. Wollestraat has some chic stores and several lace shops. You will find more touristy shops, including several selling lace, in Breidelstraat (which links Markt to Burg), just to the east of the Belfort. Hoogstraat, where there are antique and design shops, is just off Burg Square.

Callebert Interior design and gift shop. ⓐ 25 Wollestraat ⓦ www.callebert.be

Chocolaterie de Burg Sells not only chocolates, but also sweet local biscuits and other things sugary. ⓐ Burg 15 ⓣ 050 33 52 32

Deldycke Excellent, if pricey, delicatessen. ⓐ Wollestraat 23
🕿 050 33 43 35

Delvaux Sells eye-wateringly expensive but beautifully designed handbags. ⓐ corner of Wollestraat & Breidelstraat 🕿 050 49 01 31
ⓦ www.Delvaux.com

Galler Divine chocolate shop. ⓐ Steenstraat 5, just off Markt
🕿 050 61 20 62

Javana A charming store selling a good variety of coffees, teas and infusions plus coffee makers, teapots, mugs and gift boxes.
ⓐ Steenstraat 6 🕿 050 33 36 05
ⓦ www.javana.be

Oil & Vinegar Delectable Mediterranean foodstuffs.
ⓐ Geldmunstraat 11 🕿 050 34 56 50 ⓦ www.oilvinegar.com

Oliver Strelli Men's shop of the Belgian design chain.
ⓐ Geldmunstraat 19

Oliver Strelli Women's shop of the Belgian design chain.
ⓐ Eiermarkt 3

The Bottle Shop Sells hundreds of types of beer, as well as *jenever* (gin), along with t-shirts and prints. ⓐ Wollestraat 13

Tintin Shop With an array of clothing, puzzles and ornaments to satisfy even the most demanding Tintin fan. ⓐ Steenstraat 3
🕿 050 33 42 92 ⓦ www.tintinshopbrugge.be

⬆ At the centre of Burg is the Stadhuis (City Hall)

TAKING A BREAK

Apart from a great little chip kiosk directly in front of the Belfort, which sells fries and accompaniments, the following are good places to eat or relax with a drink:

Häagen-Dazs £ ❶ Part of the international chain, this ice-cream shop also sells waffles, pancakes and coffee. ⓐ Wollestraat 31 ❶ 050 34 79 99

Humpty Dumpty £ ❷ Snacks, sandwiches, breakfast, pasta, waffles and ice cream. You can also get a drink or coffee. Speedy service. Eat in (including the terrace) or take-away. ⓐ Sint-Amandsstraat 35 🕐 08.30–24.00 (summer); 08.30–20.00 (winter)

Sandwicherie St-Amand £ ❸ A bright, modern place with tables outside, where you can get baguettes, soups and salads. Just off the west side of Markt. ⓐ Sint-Amandsstraat 38 🕒 09.30–18.30

Pili Pili £–££ ❹ A pleasant, modern café in a 17th-century house which serves pasta and other Italian and Mediterranean-inspired food. ⓐ Hoogstraat 17 🕿 050 49 11 49 🕒 12.00–14.30 & 18.00–22.30

Vineeto £–££ ❺ A wine bar serving tapas and Belgian specialities, in a road behind the Belfort. ⓐ Oude Burg 10 🕒 11.00–23.00 Wed–Sat, 17.00–23.00 Sun & Tues, closed Mon

Craenenburg ££ ❻ Not cheap to eat, due to its great location, but very good for food in large portions, and one of only two places on Markt that are frequented by locals. Good sandwiches and an interior with stained-glass windows illustrating brewing. Drink prices are reasonable. ⓐ Markt 16 🕿 050 33 34 02 🕒 07.30–24.00

Den Gouden Karpel ££ ❼ An excellent and cosy fish and seafood restaurant near the Vismarkt (fish market) with a terrace, and a shop (at Vismarkt 10) where you can buy food to take out. ⓐ Huidenvetterplein 3–4 🕿 050 33 34 94 🕒 restaurant 12.00–14.00 & 18.30–21.30 (winter); restaurant 12.00–22.00 (summer); shop 08.00–12.00 & 14.00–18.30 Tues–Sat, closed Sun & Mon

Huyze die Maene ££ ❽ The other place in Markt favoured by the locals. Excellent, well-presented food, and acceptable drinks prices. Slightly more expensive than the neighbouring Craenenburg, but you can always just have a salad or an omelette. Comfortable interior. ⓐ Markt 17 🕿 050 33 39 59 🕒 09.00–23.00

AFTER DARK

Bruges doesn't exactly buzz with activity after dark, but many bars and cafés remain open late. If you simply want to eat, you have plenty of choice, and a walk along the Gronerei Canal and Dijver is always romantic, with floodlit buildings reflected in the water. The Belfort is also floodlit, and Markt can look its best at night.

Restaurants

Bistro de Pompe £–££ ❾ Grills, salads, stir-fries and vegetarian dishes. There's a tea room where you can get snacks at lunchtime. ⓐ Kleine Sint-Amandstraat 2 ❶ 050 61 66 18 ❶ 11.30–22.00, closed Mon

Malpertuus-'t Voske £–££ ❿ It has certainly seen better days, but it serves robust, basic, French and local cuisine, including *waterzool* (chicken/fish broth) at reasonable prices. ⓐ Eiermarkt 9 ❶ 050 33 30 38 ❶ 12.00–14.00 & 18.00–22.30

Opus Latino Eetcafe £–££ ⓫ Fashionable and popular, with a terrace. It serves tapas, snacks, pasta and salads. ⓐ Burg 15 ❶ 050 34 72 78 ❶ 10.30–01.00, closed Wed

't Dreveken £–££ ⓬ Flemish cuisine, with a canal view if you're lucky, in a 17th-century building. ⓐ Huidenvettersplein 10 ❶ 050 33 95 06 ❶ 12.00–14.30 & 18.00–22.00 Mon & Wed–Fri, 12.00–22.00 Sat & Sun, closed Tues

❶ *Look up to appreciate the opulence of the Stadhuis' council chamber*

Breydel-De Coninc ££ ⓭ Family-run for over 40 years (it started as a café), this friendly place is a favourite with both locals and tourists. The speciality is mussels – cooked in nine different ways – as well as other seafood and *waterzool* (chicken/fish broth). It's between Markt and Burg. ⓐ Breidelstraat 24 ⓣ 050 33 97 46 ⓛ 12.00–15.00 & 18.00–22.00, last orders 21.30, closed Wed

Calis ££ ⓮ A superior restaurant with a pleasant décor and ambience which serves French and Mediterranean food. ⓐ Hoogstraat 10 ⓣ 050 61 31 81 ⓛ 12.00–14.00 & 19.00–02.00, closed Tues & Wed

Den Amand ££ ⓯ A small and cosy restaurant just off Markt, much liked by locals, serving a range of international dishes. ⓐ Sint-Amandstraat 4 ⓣ 050 34 01 22 ⓛ 12.00–13.45 & 18.00–21.45, closed Mon (and Wed in winter)

De Stove ££ ⓰ A very good, elegant, family-run restaurant (he cooks, she serves), with a small but tempting menu of French and Belgian dishes. ⓐ Kleine Sint-Amandstraat 4 ⓣ 050 33 78 35 ⓛ 12.00–13.45 (except Wed, Thur & Fri) & 18.45–21.30, closed two weeks in Jan & June

Duc de Bourgogne ££ ⓱ Formal, old-fashioned ambience and traditional food, but romantic, and great canal views from the best tables. There are also a few bedrooms. ⓐ Huidenvettersplein 12 ⓣ 050 33 20 38 ⓛ closed lunchtime Mon & Tues

't Bezemtje ££ ⓲ Warm and rustic, serving rich, high-quality cuisine. ⓐ Kleine Sint-Amandsstraat 1 ⓣ 050 33 91 68 ⓛ 18.30–21.30, closed Sun & Mon

Red! ££–£££ ⑱ A trendy spot with modern design and light, contemporary cooking. ⓐ Vlamingstraat 53 ⓣ 050 61 40 06 ⓛ 11.30–14.00 & 18.30–23.00, closed Thur

Bars & clubs
Charlie Rockets The bar of this lively hostel gets full quickly. You can get something simple to eat early on, and then stay till late in the night. ⓐ Hoogstraat 19 ⓣ 050 33 06 60

There is hardly anywhere to dance in Bruges, but **De Coulissen** (ⓐ Jacob van Oostraat 4) and **De Korrekelder** (ⓐ Kraanplein 6) are your best bet.

Kaffee l'aMaRal A clubby feel and contemporary music. ⓐ Kuiperstraat 10

Plantenmarkt Just off Markt. ⓐ Sint-Amandstraat 2 ⓣ 050 33 29 64

Relax A cocktail bar with R&B playing. ⓐ Sint-Jakobstraat 45

Staminee de Garre A beer bar which serves snacks. ⓐ De Garre 1 ⓣ 050 34 10 29 ⓛ 12.00–24.00 Mon & Tues, 12.00–01.00 Fri, 11.00–01.00 Sat, 11.00–24.00 Sun

Vuurmolen A young crowd with all-night staying power. ⓐ Kraanplein 5 ⓣ 050 33 00 79

Zwart Huis Jazz in the background in a building dating from the 15th century. Very popular so it gets crowded. You can also eat here. ⓐ Kuiperstraat 23 ⓣ 050 34 15 16

South of Markt

The great majority of Bruges' main attractions lie south of Markt. It is only around 2.6 km (1⅔ miles) from east to west, and 1.5 km (1 mile) from Markt to the southern limits of the old city. So it is easy to walk around and see almost all of it if you are in Bruges even just for a couple of days. Apart from Markt, this area is likely to be where you will spend most of your time in Bruges. If you can recognise the Church of Our Lady and St Saviour's Cathedral, as well as the Belfort, you shouldn't get lost or go far off track.

SIGHTS & ATTRACTIONS

Even if you don't have time to enter all the museums, the buildings themselves, their grounds and the canals around them provide attractive walking routes. The most appealing are the grounds of **Sint-Janshospitaal**, the **Arentshuis** and the **Begijnhof**. It is also worth walking around the outside of the **Concertgebouw**, even if you never listen to a concert there or visit an exhibition. The Concertgebouw is at one end of the busy **'t Zand Square**, where there is a large market on Saturdays, and next to the main bus station of the town centre.

The area also has small parks – **Minnewaterpark**, **Astridpark** and **Koning Albertpark** – and other open spaces to relax in.

CULTURE

Archaeology Museum
Part of the Sint-Janshospitaal complex (see page 82), the museum's entrance is also in Mariastraat. This is an ingenious, modern

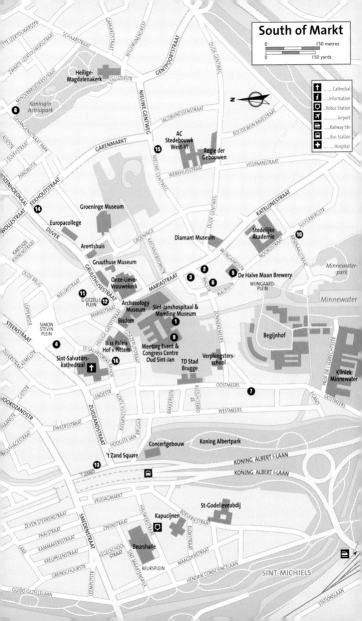

South of Markt

0 — 150 metres
0 — 150 yards

✝	......Cathedral
ℹ	......Information
⊙	......Police Station
✈	......Airport
🚆	......Railway Stn
🚌	......Bus Station
✚	......Hospital

Heilige-Magdalenakerk
Koningin Astridpark
8
SLUZENSTR
GABRIELSTRAAT
WILLEMSWINDREEF
OUDE GENTWEG
SCHAARSTRAAT
'TTE LEERTOUWERSSTR
ZWARTE LEERTOUWERSSTR
MINDERBROEDERSSTRAAT
GEVANGENISSTRAAT PARK
ALSSKO
PANDREITJE
OZENHOEDKAAI
EEKHOUTSTRAAT
WOLLESTRAAT
14
NIEUWE GENTWEG
JACOBINESSENSTRAAT
GARENMARKT
BOUDEWIJN RAVESTRAAT
VISSPAANSTRAAT
WERKHUISSTRAAT
15 AC Stedebouwk West-VI
Regie der Gebouwen
Groeninge Museum
Europacollege
Arentshuis
Gruuthuse Museum
Onze-Lieve-Vrouwekerk
DIJVER
GROENINGE
KASTANJEBOOMSTR
MARIASTRAAT
Diamant Museum
WIJNGAARDSTR
Stedelijke Academie
10
KATELIJNESTRAAT
SULFERBERGSTR
NOORDSTRAAT
ARSENAALSTRAAT
Minnewater-park
KARTUIZE
RINNELSTRAAT
OUDE BRUG
NIEUWSTRAAT
GRUUTHUSESTRAAT
11 G Gezelle Plein **12**
Archaeology Museum
Bisdom
Sint-Janshospitaal & Memling Museum
3 **2** **6**
WALSTR
WALPLEIN
5 De Halve Maan Brewery
WIJNGAARD-PLEIN
Minnewater
ZONNEKEMEERS
Begijnhof
SIMON STEVIN PLEIN
4
MARIASTRAAT
HEILIGE GEESTSTRAAT
OOSTMEERS
Biss Paleis Hof v Pittem
16
Meeting Event & Congress Centre Oud Sint-Jan
9
TD Stad Brugge
Verpleegstersschool
KLINIEK MINNEWATER
Kliniek Minnewater
PROF DR J SEBRECHTSSTR
EILAND
OOSTMEERS
Sint-Salvators-kathedraal ✝
STEENSTRAAT
ZILVERSTRAAT
GEISTE
ZILVERPAND
LENDESTR
KORTE VULDERSTR
 ST OBRECHTSTR
BAKKERSTR
OOSTMEERS
WESTMEERS
SINT-SALVATORSKHOF
NOORDZANDSTR
HAANTJE
WULFHAGESTRAAT
DWEERSSTRAAT
ZUIDZANDSTRAAT
HOOGSTE VAN
VRIJDAGMARKT
Concertgebouw
't Zand Square
13
't ZAND
Koning Albertpark
KONING ALBERT I-LAAN
KONING ALBERT I-LAAN
ZEVEN STERRENSTRAAT
PAALSTRAAT
KAMMAKERSSTRAAT
KREUPELENSTRAAT
SMEDENSTRAAT
ZWIJNSTRAAT
HAUWERSTRAAT
KEGELSCHOOL STRAAT
Kapucijnen
BOEVERIESTRAAT
St-Godelieveabdij
KLOKSTRAAT
GREINSCHUURSTR
GUIDO GEZELLELAAN
LANE
GUIDO GEZELLELAAN
LEAPLEISTRAAT
ST MAKERISTRAAT
Beurshalle
BEURSPLEIN
MAAGDENSTRAAT
HENDRIK CONSCIENCELAAN
SINT-MICHIELS
STATIONSPLN

museum which is lively and fun for both children and adults, with many interactive displays.

ⓐ Mariastraat 36a ⓦ www.brugge.be ⓛ 09.30–12.30 & 13.30–17.00, closed Mon; small admission charge

Arentshuis (Brangwyn Museum)

The Arentshuis was originally built in 1663. The building was given its current neoclassical look by its owner in the late 18th century, including features such as the ancient-Egyptian-style pillars at the front, the fireplaces and the pretty staircase. It was a private house until 1908, and is named after its last proprietor, Aquilin Arents de Beertegem. It is now owned by the city.

The Brangwyn collection is housed upstairs, and there are regular temporary exhibitions on the ground floor. Bruges-born British artist Frank Brangwyn (1867–1956) donated many of his vivid paintings, and some of the furniture he designed, to the city of Bruges in the 1930s. He was the son of William Brangwyn, an architect and designer who was among the many British enthusiasts who helped to restore Bruges in neo-Gothic style in the 19th century.

The house is in the grounds of Arentspark – a good spot to chill out in and take a break from pounding the streets and museums. The park has one of Bruges' prettiest bridges, and sculptures by the Belgian Rik Poot.

ⓐ Dijver 16 ⓦ www.brugge.be ⓛ 09.30–17.00, closed Mon (except Easter & Whit Mon); small admission charge, or included in the admission charge to Groeninge Museum

Begijnhof (Beguinage)

Beguines were single women who led a religious life in communities such as the one that once inhabited the Begijnhof, founded in 1245.

They were often the widows of men who had died in the Crusades. Many beguines returned to life outside in due course.

They lived in the delightful rows of small, whitewashed houses, dating from the 17th and 18th centuries, which you will see. There is also a garden in the middle of the compound, which is particularly

◔ *The Begijnhof was once the domain of religious single women*

attractive in spring, and a church (1602). One of the houses, just inside the gate to the left, serves as a museum of the lives led in the Begijnhof.

The houses are now occupied by elderly local ladies, usually widows. A community of Benedictine nuns also live in the enclave.

The Begijnhof is one of Bruges' most peaceful spots. There is a small entry charge for the museum, but none for the compound as a whole.

ⓐ Begijnhof 30 ⓦ www.brugge.be ⓛ museum 10.00–12.00 & 13.45–17.00 Mon–Sat, 10.45–12.00 & 13.45–17.00 Sun

Concertgebouw

You will either love or hate Bruges' massive new concert hall, completed when Bruges was named European City of Culture in 2002. Either you will think it is a blot on the landscape, as many locals did, or you will think that it is an innovative and imaginatively designed breath of fresh air in a place that perhaps otherwise trades too much on its medieval past. Faced with 68,000 terracotta tiles, it's undeniably noticeable, stretching 120 m (393 ft) from end to end. The colour of the tiles is characteristic of many of Bruges' buildings. Whatever your opinion, it has made an important contribution to the local cultural scene with a concert hall seating 1,300 people and a chamber music hall seating 320. Contemporary art shows are also put on at the top of the building, from where you can get great views of Bruges. The tourist office (In&Uit Brugge) is situated in the building, and you can buy tickets there, and get information about events and exhibitions not only in the Concertgebouw but also elsewhere in Bruges.

ⓐ 't Zand 34 ⓣ 050 47 69 99 ⓦ www.concertgebouw.be ⓛ tourist office 10.00–18.00 Fri–Wed, 10.00–20.00 Thur

De Halve Maan Brewery

This family-owned brewery (the name means 'half moon') has been going since 1856. Here you can learn all about how the drink is made by taking one of the guided tours which leave on the hour and last 45 minutes. A free glass of their new beer, Brugse Zot, is included in the visit. If you don't want to go on the tour, the brewery has a café where you can try a glass of its brown or blonde beer (Straffe Hendrick or 'strong Henry'), or have a coffee and snack.

ⓐ Walplein 26 ⓣ 050 33 26 97 ⓦ www.halvemaan.be ⓛ tours hourly 11.00–16.00 Mon–Fri, 11.00–17.00 Sat & Sun (summer); 11.00–15.00 Mon–Fri, 11.00–16.00 Sat & Sun (winter); admission charge for tour

Diamant Museum (Diamond Museum)

Diamonds are an important export for Belgium, and this privately owned museum tells the history of Bruges and its connection with the gem. It is thought that the skill of diamond polishing actually originated in Bruges 500 years ago, when it was a more important diamond centre than Amsterdam or Antwerp. The museum is well-organised and surprisingly interesting. Look out for the uncut 250-carat diamond on show. There is a diamond-polishing demonstration at 12.15 every day, which costs extra.

ⓐ Katelijnestraat 43 ⓣ 050 34 20 56 ⓦ www.diamondmuseum.be ⓛ 10.00–17.30, closed Christmas Day & New Year's Day; admission charge

Groeninge Museum

This museum houses one of the finest collections of Flemish art in the world – spanning 600 years from the 15th century to the present day – arranged chronologically from room to room and beautifully displayed.

Highlights include Jan van Eyck's stunningly detailed *Virgin and Child with Canon Joris van der Paele* (1436), Hugo van der Goes' emotional and modern-looking *Death of the Virgin* (1481), Hans Memling's *Triptych of Willem Moreel* (1484) and *The Last Judgement*, attributed to Hieronymus Bosch (early 16th century).

Although the Groeninge isn't huge, if you're short of time concentrate on the first five rooms, which contain the finest works. Room 9 has a Magritte and other Surrealist works.

ⓐ Dijver 12 ⓦ www.brugge.be ⓒ 09.30–17.00, closed Mon; admission charge includes audioguide and entry to Arentshuis Museum

◯ *The pretty courtyard at the pharmacy of Sint-Janshospitaal*

Gruuthuse Museum

The Gruuthuse is essentially an attempt to show how the wealthy of Bruges lived when the city was at its most prosperous. The huge house, one of the top six historical sites in Bruges and so under the Bruggemuseum umbrella, was much restored in the late 19th and early 20th century. It was originally the residence of the Flemish knight, Louis (or Lodewijk) van Gruuthuse. It now houses a collection of art and domestic artefacts.

Many of the objects – which include furniture, paintings, tapestries and musical instruments – are lovely and finely crafted. But equally impressive are the wooden ceilings, floor tiles, carvings and vast fireplaces. The huge kitchen is another highlight.

Perhaps the most unexpected exhibit is the guillotine (on the ground floor), which first beheaded a criminal in the Markt in 1796, and was last used in 1862.

❸ Dijver 17 ⓦ www.brugge.be ⓛ 09.30–17.00, closed Mon; admission charge includes audioguide and entry to the museum in the Church of Our Lady

Onze-Lieve-Vrouwekerk (Church of Our Lady)

The 122-m (400-ft) spire of this enormous Gothic church dominates the skyline of the area, and can scarcely be missed. Part of the Bruggemuseum, one of the six most important historical sites in Bruges, it took 200 years to build, from 1220 onwards, and the spire was completed by 1350. As with so many buildings in Bruges, the interior, much of it surprisingly light, has a mixture of architectural styles. The simple central aisle dates from the 13th century, and the north aisle from the 14th century, but there are also baroque side chapels, and an ostentatious pulpit dating from 1743.

The church's main highlight, at the end of the south aisle, is Michelangelo's exquisite *Madonna and Child* sculpture (1504), one of the very few outside Italy, donated to the church by a local merchant in 1514. If you have time, the church's museum is worth a visit.
ⓐ Mariastraat ⓣ 050 34 53 14 ⓛ 09.30–16.50 Mon–Sat, 13.30–16.50 Sun, museum closed Mon

Sint-Janshospitaal (St John's Hospital) & Memling Museum

Just across the road from the Church of Our Lady, the Sint-Janshospitaal site is one of the biggest in Bruges, and once you enter the archway on Mariastraat, you will find a haven of calm – along with some shops, the internet café, Coffee Link, and a restaurant.

The hospital functioned from 1150 to as late as 1976. The main buildings on Mariastraat date from the 13th century. At that time the hospital was at the edge of the city. The complex once housed a church, convent, bakery, brewery, vegetable garden, and other facilities for the sick. Those who lived there devoted themselves to both healing and God. Much of the original was demolished in 1850.

The Memling Museum, housed in the old wards (entrance on Mariastraat) is an imaginative conversion of the ancient space. The museum is essentially in two parts, one showing the past life of the hospital and Bruges itself (with interactive terminals), including documents, works of art, furniture and other artefacts. The other, in the chapel, shows six works by the Flemish master Hans Memling (1440–94), of whom the hospital was a major patron. All the Memling paintings on display are remarkable, but the highlight is the triptych of *St John the Baptist and St John the Evangelist* (1479). You have only to look at any of the Memling works on display, and compare them to the other early Flemish works in the museum, to appreciate what a master of colour, composition and detail he was.

Don't miss the hospital's 17th-century pharmacy, which was originally run by nuns and kept on dispensing until 1971. Situated just to the right of the arch leading in to the hospital complex, is an array of old drug and herb jars in a building with a pretty courtyard. ⓐ Mariastraat 38 ⓒ museum 09.30–17.00; pharmacy 09.30–11.45 & 14.00–17.00, closed Mon; admission charge includes audioguide

RETAIL THERAPY

If it's clothes you want, head to the area around St-Saviour's Cathedral, particularly Steenstraat, but also Zuidzandstraat, Noordzandstraat and Zilverpand (where there are several boutiques). Many of the international chains are located there, as well as Belgian fashion shops, and you'll also find some good chocolate shops. The Saturday market on 't Zand sells both cheap clothes and food, though the quality of the clothes is nothing to write home about. Katelijnestraat and its continuation Mariastraat also have numerous shops, many of which sell souvenirs and are strictly touristy, but there are some decent chocolate shops and others.

There is a flea market along the Dijver all week during summer and at weekends in winter, depending on the weather. But you will be disappointed if you expect to find some lovely little antique or amusing piece of bric-a-brac there: most of the goods on sale are new and of doubtful quality. Shops to look out for include:

Bilbo One of the best CD shops in town, with very reasonable prices. ⓐ Noordzandstraat 82 ⓣ 050 33 40 11

Chocolaterie Sukerbuyc One of the best chocolate shops in Bruges. ⓐ Katelijnestraat 5 ⓣ 050 33 08 87

Confisserie Zucchero A new chocolate and sweet shop where you can see the confections being made. ⓐ Mariastraat 18 ⓣ 050 33 39 62

Dille en Kamille Sells crockery and other household goods at competitive prices. ⓐ Simon Stevin Plein 17–18 ⓣ 050 34 11 80

Knapp Targa One of Bruges' most stylish fashion shops.
ⓐ Zuidzandstraat 22 ⓣ 050 33 31 27

Neuhaus Another very good Belgian chocolate chain, considered by many to be the best. ⓐ Steenstraat 73 ⓣ 050 33 15 30

Quicke Bruges' leading shop for fashion shoes, including top international brands. ⓐ Zuidzandstraat 21 ⓣ 050 33 23 00

The Bear Necessities A pretty teddy-bear shop, just behind Arentspark. ⓐ Groeninge 23 ⓣ 050 34 10 27

TAKING A BREAK

The area south of Markt has numerous tea rooms, cafés and small restaurants where you can get something to eat. There are clusters of them near all the main sights, particularly the Church of Our Lady, and around Begijnhof. Some restaurants in the area double up as tea rooms in the afternoon, and you can get light meals or a drink there after around 14.00, usually until 18.00. The many restaurants and bars on 't Zand Square tend to be expensive.

ⓞ *The Church of Our Lady's Gothic façade is a dominating sight*

The Coffee Link £ ❶ One of Bruges' few internet cafés, and the easiest to find. Within the precincts of the Sint-Janshospitaal complex. ⓐ Mariastraat 38 ⓣ 050 34 99 73 ⓛ 11.00–18.00, closed Wed

De Bron £ ❷ One of Bruges' very few vegetarian restaurants. ⓐ Katelijnestraat 82 ⓣ 050 33 45 26 ⓛ 11.45–14.00, closed Sun & Mon

De Proverie £ ❸ The tea room of the Sukerbuyc chocolate shop opposite, and popular with locals. It boasts the only real English tea in Bruges. ⓐ Katelijnestraat 6

Jerry's Cigar Bar £ ❹ Sells not only cigars and cigarettes, but also has a small (and necessarily smoky) modern café at the back where you can get a drink and very good ice creams, but not much else in the way of food. ⓐ Simon Stevin Plein 13 ⓣ 050 33 77 94 ⓦ www.jerrycigarbar.com ⓛ 08.00–19.00 Mon–Sat, 10.00–19.00 Sun

De Halve Maan Brewery £–££ ❺ Snacks, drinks (including beer) and fuller meals are available at the brewery's café. ⓐ Walplein 26 ⓣ 050 33 26 97 ⓛ until 18.00

Begijntje ££ ❻ Opposite the De Halve Maan brewery, a restaurant and tea room, where you can sit outside. ⓐ Walstraat 11 ⓣ 050 33 00 89 ⓛ closed Tues & Wed

De Stoepa ££ ❼ Dishes from around the world in this café near the Begijnhof. ⓐ Oostmeers 124 ⓣ 050 33 04 54 ⓛ closed Mon

L'Estaminet ££ ❽ A lively place, with occasional live music, just off Astridpark. Known for its pasta. ⓐ Park 5 ⓣ 050 34 40 52

AFTER DARK

It gets quieter and quieter after dark the further south you go from Markt. There are just a few bars, and most of the better restaurants cluster around Dijver and the Church of Our Lady. A walk along the Dijver, where many of the buildings are floodlit, is one of the delights of Bruges.

Restaurants

B-In ££ ⑨ A cool new restaurant, with a huge bar area (where you can get snacks), with ultra-modern design, a relaxed ambience and a young clientele. The food is creative, contemporary, beautifully presented and of very high quality. There is a terrace on a canal in daytime. You get there by walking through the Sint-Janshospitaal complex. ⓐ Oud Sint-Jan ☏ 050 31 13 00 ⏰ 12.00–14.30 & 18.30–22.00

De Bekoring ££ ⑩ A romantic restaurant, near Minnewaterpark, with a fireplace and candlelight in the evening. Good local cuisine. ⓐ Arsenaalstraat 55 ☏ 050 34 41 57 ⏰ 12.00–14.00 & 16.30–21.30, closed Sun evening, Mon & Tues

Maria van Bourgondië ££ ⑪ Good, authentic Burgundian and Flemish cuisine in an elegant, old-fashioned atmosphere (beamed ceiling, chandeliers, panelled walls) at the end of Dijver. There is a terrace outside where you can get tea, a drink or a light meal during the day. ⓐ Guido Gezelleplein 1 ☏ 050 33 20 68 ⏰ 09.00–23.00

Marieke van Brugghe ££ ⑫ Opposite the Onze-Lieve-Vrouwekerk (Church of Our Lady), this traditional restaurant serving French and

Flemish food specialises in meat, particularly steaks, but also serves fish and oysters. The classic menu is good value. It is a tea room during the afternoon. It has outside tables. 🄰 Mariastraat 17 🅣 050 34 33 66 🅛 12.00–21.30

't Putje ££ ⓭ A hotel with a cosy restaurant and decent food. Prices are reasonable, particularly at lunchtime when you can get a light meal. 🄰 't Zand 31 🅣 050 33 28 47 🅛 11.00–23.00

Den Dyver ££–£££ ⓮ One of Bruges' smartest and best-regarded restaurants serving imaginative food cooked with beer. Beer is matched to the dishes and served in wine glasses. Whatever you choose from the menu, you're in for an interesting experience. 🄰 Dijver 5 🅣 050 33 60 69 🅛 closed Wed & Thur lunch

De Snippe ££–£££ ⓯ Part of a hotel and one of the city's foremost gastronomic restaurants, with an attractive winter garden and terrace. There is also a vegetarian menu. Near Astridpark. 🄰 Nieuwe Gentweg 53 🅣 050 33 70 70 🅛 12.00–14.30 & 19.00–21.30, closed Sun & Mon lunch

Kardinaalshof ££–£££ ⓰ Smart gastronomic restaurant in a 19th-century house, specialising in fish and seafood. Near St Saviour's Cathedral. 🄰 Sint-Salvatorskerkhof 14 🅣 050 34 16 91 🅛 12.00–14.00 & 19.00–21.30, closed Tues lunch & Wed, and first two weeks in July

Bars & pubs

B-In The bar in this restaurant (see page 87) buzzes after 23.00 and stays that way until 03.00, with a DJ and a fantastic sound system (but no dancing).

De Lokkedize A bar near the Church of Our Lady. Unusually, you can actually punctuate the drinking with a well-made snack here as well. ⓐ Korte Vulderstraat 33 ⓣ 050 33 44 50

Joey's A welcoming bar with good music. ⓐ Zuidzandstraat 160 ⓣ 050 34 12 64

't Brugs Beertje One of the best beer pubs in Bruges, usually packed and very friendly. It serves around 300 types of beer, and is open late at the weekend. Ask their advice if you don't know what to drink. ⓐ Kemelstraat 5, off Steenstraat ⓣ 050 33 96 16

⬤ *Choosing between all the beers on offer can be difficult!*

Northeast of Markt

The area north and east of Markt won't necessarily be top of your agenda to visit if you are in Bruges for just a day or two, but it is peaceful and very attractive to walk through, with a number of quiet canals, pocket-sized squares, notable churches and a handful of small museums. This is particularly true of the St Anna district, once the poorer part of town, and almost entirely residential, consisting of streets with small cottages, often with stained-glass mullioned windows. There are few shops, bars or restaurants there. Then again, it is the least touristy part of Bruges, and well away from most of the crowds. If you take a canal-boat ride, it will take you along St Anna Canal (Sint-Annarei) for part of the way. You'll probably only want to go there during daylight hours, but sunset along the canals in the area is a sight worth waiting for.

SIGHTS & ATTRACTIONS

If you leave Markt and go along Vlamingstraat, you will pass the impressive **Stadsschouwburg** (City Theatre), built in 1868 in neoclassical style. A little further along, you will come to the much-restored **Ter Beurze** house (ⓐ Vlamingstraat 35), dating from the 14th century, and the site of the world's first stock exchange. The family that owned it (van der Beurse) gave their name to the term 'bourse' that is used for many of the world's stock exchanges today. The area near the Ter Beurze house was where many foreign merchants based themselves when Bruges was a centre of commerce in the 14th and 15th centuries. Next to the Ter Beurze house (No. 37) is the site of what used to be the Venetian trading lodge (or consulate) in the Middle Ages. It is now a bookshop. At the beginning of **Acadamiestraat** (No. 1)

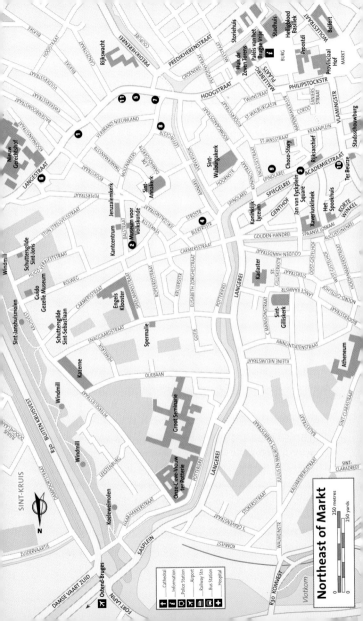

Northeast of Markt

0   250 metres

0   250 yards

Cathedral
Information
Police Station
Airport
Railway Stn
Bus Station
Hospital

was the Florentine lodge – now the fashionable De Florentijnen restaurant. Spanjaardstraat, which leads off Acadamiestraat, was where Spanish merchants lived. Continuing along Acadamiestraat, you will get to **Jan van Eyckplein**, a lovely, small, cobbled square with benches, on the Spiegelrei Canal. The statue of the great Flemish painter Jan van Eyck was erected here in the 19th century. If you keep walking along **Spiegelrei**, you will come across the sites of more foreign merchants' lodges. Spiegelrei 15, for instance, was the English lodge in the 15th century. Further along the canal (just off Langerei) is **Sint-Gilliskerk**, the church where Hans Memling is buried. Alternatively, you can cross the canal to the St Anna district once you get to the bridge at Genthof. A more direct route to St Anna from Markt is to go via the Burg and Hoogstraat, and cross the canal there.

CULTURE

Choco-Story
Prepare to drool. This private museum is understandably popular with both adults and children, and is usually packed. It is well thought out and tells the story of chocolate from its origins in Maya and Aztec civilisations, to the chocolate trade and how chocolate is processed, to Belgian chocolate, and finally a chocolate-making demonstration on the ground floor. By the time visitors reach the museum's shop at the end of the tour, only the hardiest of souls are able to resist the fragrant temptations that present themselves. There are several fascinating exhibits along the way on the museum's three floors, and also a film about chocolate. As you enter you will see a fabulously giant 120-kg (264-lb) Easter egg.
ⓐ Wijnzakstraat 2, Sint-Jansplein ⓣ 050 61 22 37 ⓦ www.choco-story.be ⓛ 10.00–17.00, closed most of Jan; admission charge

Engels Klooster (English Convent)

A surprisingly large, domed building, which gets its name from the
time that English Catholics fled to the Spanish Netherlands in the

⬤ *The Choco-Story museum explains how cocoa was once used as currency*

16th century. The refugees included nuns, who founded this
establishment in 1629. Later, the exiled Charles II (who lived in
Bruges in 1656–9 before his restoration to the English throne)
prayed here. The interior, dating from the 18th century, is essentially
baroque. The place once housed a boarding school for English
Catholic girls, and nuns still live there. Check opening times with the
tourist office; the convent isn't officially open to the public, but
visitors are often allowed in at specified times.

ⓐ Carmersstraat 85 ⓣ 050 33 24 24 ⓦ www.brugge.be ⓛ usually
14.00–16.00 & 16.30–17.30, closed first Sun of the month

Guido Gezelle Museum

Guido Gezelle (1830–99) was one of Flanders' best known poets (there is
even a small square named after him at one end of Dijver), and the brick
house in which he was born, with its large, pleasing garden, is now a
museum dedicated to him and his work. Gezelle, a major figure in Dutch
literature, was also a priest. His use of Dutch, when educated Belgium
was dominated by French speakers, makes him something of a Flemish
hero. The house will give you a good impression of how people lived in
19th-century Bruges.

ⓐ Rolweg 64 ⓦ www.brugge.be ⓛ 09.30–12.30 & 13.30–17.00, closed
Mon; small admission charge

Jeruzalemkerk (Jerusalem Church) and Kantcentrum (Lace Centre)

The Jerusalem Church is a most unusual one, with a Byzantine look,
quite unlike any other in the city. It was built by the Genoese
Adornes (or Adorno) family in the 15th century, after a pilgrimage by
one of them to Jerusalem. The interior is equally bizarre, with part of
it based on the Holy Sepulchre in Jerusalem. There are skulls on the
altarpiece (symbolising Golgotha) and the black marble tomb of

Anselm Adornes (which contains only his heart), from which a sword hilt emerges to symbolise his murder in Scotland in 1483. The 16th-century stained-glass windows immortalise the history of the family. The church is still owned by the descendants of its founders.

The Lace Centre is just next door in a row of almshouses. There are some outstanding examples of old hand-made lace in the many forms in which it has been used, both in the home and in fashion. The thing to catch, however, is the lace-making demonstration (14.00 onwards) in the Adornes' former house.

ⓐ Peperstraat 3 ⓣ 050 33 00 72 ⓦ kantcentrum.com ⓛ 10.00–12.00 & 14.00–18.00 Mon–Fri, 10.00–12.00 & 14.00–17.00 Sat, closed Sun; small admission charge includes church and Lace Centre

Onze-Lieve-Vrouw ter Potterie (Our Lady of the Pottery)

The hospital of Our Lady of the Pottery, served by monks and nuns, was founded here in 1276, and a church was added in the next century. It was renovated in fancy baroque style in the 17th century and contains a statue of the Virgin and Child – venerated by some as miraculous – and some good 17th-century tapestries. The hospital was eventually converted into an old people's home, and the elderly still live in buildings in the grounds. The old wards are now a museum containing a collection of art, religious objects, relics of the hospital and other exhibits. The whole place has a pleasant ambience.

ⓐ Potterierei 79 ⓣ 050 44 87 11 ⓦ www.brugge.be ⓛ 09.30–12.30 & 13.30–17.00, closed Mon; small admission charge

Sint-Annakerk (St Anna Church)

A key landmark in the district (recognisable by its slender spire), the St Anna Church is the parish church for the area and has a charm that few other churches in Bruges can match. Although originally finished in 1497, it was destroyed by arson in 1591 during the Wars of Religion and, as a result, the interior dates from the 17th and 18th centuries, untouched by the neo-Gothic revival in the city. The painting of *The Last Judgement* over the entrance, by Hendrik Herregouts, is the biggest in Bruges.

📍 Sint-Annaplein 🌐 www.brugge.be 🕐 10.00–12.00 & 14.00–17.00 Mon–Sat, 14.00–17.00 Sun (summer), closed winter

Sint-Walburgakerk

One of the gems of Bruges, and not often visited by tourists, this church was built for Jesuits in 1619–43, and is huge, light, peaceful and very uplifting. Music often plays in the background even when there is no service. With a black-and-white marble interior and an impressive organ, the church (apart from the altar) is much less ornate than you might expect of a baroque building. It forms an interesting contrast in a city with so many Gothic and neo-Gothic buildings. It's not far from Markt Square (and Choco-Story), so it's no huge effort to visit, and it's rewarding when you get there. It's a short walk from the church to the St Anna district.

📍 Sint-Maartensplein 🌐 www.brugge.be 🕐 10.00–12.00 & 14.00–17.00 Mon–Sat, 14.00–17.00 Sun (summer), closed winter

Museum voor Volkskunde (Folklore Museum)

The thought of going to a folklore museum might not sound incredibly exciting, but this one, in a terrace of 17th-century almshouses once belonging to the cobbler's guild, is worth the trip. Actually, the museum hasn't much to do with folklore, and is almost entirely concerned with the various traditional shops and crafts – such as leatherwork, hat-making, confectionery and a pharmacy –

that were once found in the city. The displays are vivid (sometimes actual shop interiors have been reconstructed) and there are demonstrations of some of the crafts (such as sweet-making 🕒 12.00–16.00 Thur). There is a congenial courtyard, and a small café/bar where you can take a break from culture and enjoy some self-indulgence instead.

ⓐ Balstraat 43 ⓦ www.brugge.be 🕒 09.30–17.00, closed Mon (except Easter & Whit Mon); small admission charge includes entry to either one of the windmills or the Guido Gezellemuseum

Windmills of the Kruisvest

The city's outer ramparts (Kruisvest) had a string of over 20 windmills along them from the 13th century until the 19th century. Now there are only four, two of which are open to the public and in working order. The Sint-Janshuismolen dates from 1770 and is the only one in its original position. The other one open to the public is Koeleweimolen. You can get good views of the surrounding area from both windmills. The Kruisvest itself, with the canal running along it, often carrying long barges, is worth walking along. One of the massive old city gates, Kruisport, built in 1403, is near the Sint-Janshuismolen.

ⓐ Kruisvest ⓦ www.brugge.be 🕒 Sint-Janshuismolen 09.30–12.30 & 13.30–17.00 Apr–Sept (weekends only Apr & Sept), Koeleweimolen 09.30–12.30 & 13.30–17.00 July–Aug, both closed Mon; small admission charge

RETAIL THERAPY

There aren't many notable shops in the area, other than in Hoogstraat and a few in Vlamingstraat and Acadamiestraat. There are also some good places to browse in Langestraat. But you might find the following of interest:

Art & Living Antique and decoration shop. ⓐ Hoogstraat 38
ⓣ 050 33 86 29

Artessuto Cushions and tapestries. ⓐ Hoedenmakersstraat 30
ⓣ 050 34 88 11

Bacchus Cornelius Sells over 400 types of Belgian beer. The same family owns the chocolate and sweet shop next door, one of Bruges' oldest. ⓐ Academiestraat 17 ⓣ 050 34 53 38

⬥ *Bruges has been heavily restored to its former glory*

De Roode Steen Leading interiors shop in a 15th-century house.
🅐 Jan van Eyckplein 8 🕐 050 33 61 51

Joaquim & Jofre Exclusive women's fashions. 🅐 Vlamingstraat 7

Sweet Moment A wide selection of chocolates and cookies.
🅐 Hoogstraat 47 🕐 050 43 12 32

TAKING A BREAK

Frituur 't Bootje £ ❶ Essentially a chip shop, and one of Bruges'
best, it also sells stews, kebabs and cold dishes. 🅐 Langestraat 91
🕐 11.30–14.00 & 17.00–24.00 Sun, Mon, Wed & Thur, 17.00–02.00 Fri
& Sat, closed Tues

Museum voor Volkskunde £ ❷ You can get a snack or a drink here
during museum opening times (see pages 96–7 for details).

Jan van Eyck Tearoom £–££ ❸ A friendly café where you can get a
light meal and sit outside in a pretty little square. 🅐 Jan van
Eyckplein 12 🕐 050 61 01 01

Vlissinghe £–££ ❹ An inn since 1515, and supposedly Bruges' oldest,
it serves beer, wine, tea, coffee, ice creams and snacks. There is a
small garden outside. Popular with locals. 🅐 Blekersstraat 2 🕐 050
34 37 37 🕐 11.00–24.00, closed Mon, Tues & Oct–Jan

De Torre ££ ❺ Grilled food, fish, mussels and regional dishes which
you can eat on the terrace overlooking a canal. 🅐 Langestraat 8 🕐 050
34 29 46 🕐 10.00–22.00, closed Tues (except July & Aug) and Wed

AFTER DARK

Nightlife is limited around here, and you might well want to head to Markt and the area around it for more fun, but a few of Bruges' best restaurants are in the area. The liveliest street is Langestraat. And, of course, you can always enjoy a quiet walk along the canals as an alternative.

Restaurants

BauHaus £–££ ❻ Relaxed bar and bistro with regional and international dishes and a young clientele. ⓐ Langestraat 135 ⓛ bistro 18.00–23.00 Mon–Thur, 18.00–24.00 Fri & Sat, closed Sun, bar open longer

Uilenspiegel £–££ ❼ This brasserie is part of a small hotel and has a terrace overlooking a canal. It's a tea room during the afternoon, serving snacks and salads. ⓐ Langestraat 2 ⓣ 050 34 65 55 ⓛ closed Wed evening, Thur & Jan

Relais Ravenstein ££ ❽ Bruges' most modern luxury hotel also offers some of the best food in town. It actually has two chefs: one with a contemporary take on simple traditional dishes; the other with expertise in Italian and fusion food. There is an oyster and seafood bar in the summer. The quick lunch (€17) is very good value. You can sit on the terrace overlooking St Anna Canal; you can also have a drink there (moderately priced) after lunch from 15.00 to 18.00, and after 23.00, or in the bar from 11.00. ⓐ Molenmeers 11 ⓣ 050 47 69 47 ⓛ 12.00–15.00 & 18.00–23.00, kitchen closes 21.30

◀ *The 15th-century Jeruzalemkerk is still owned by descendants of its founder*

Spinola ££ A gastronomic restaurant with reasonable prices and high-quality seasonal food including game and seafood. Near Jan van Eycksplein. Good atmosphere. ⓐ Spinolarei 1 ⓣ 050 34 17 85 ⓛ 12.00–13.30 & 19.00–21.00, closed Sun, Mon lunch, late Jan & June

De Florentijnen £££ One of Bruges' most chic restaurants, split-level, with sharp and knowledgeable service, and stylish presentation of complex Italian-influenced modern dishes. An impressive wine list too. ⓐ Academiestraat 1 ⓣ 050 67 75 33 ⓛ 12.00–14.30 & 19.00–22.30, closed Sun & Mon

De Karmeliet £££ With three Michelin stars, this is one of Belgium's most famous restaurants. Superb food and service, as you would expect, in a mansion with a garden. This place is formal and jacket and tie are compulsory. ⓐ Langestraat 19 ⓣ 050 33 82 59 ⓛ 12.00–14.00 & 19.00–22.00 Wed–Sat, closed Tues lunch & Sun evening

Bars
De Kelk Actually three bars (including the Wunderbar, where you can try a range of Belgian beers). Parties and gigs are often held here. Very young and lively, with dancing to music from the 70s, 80s and 90s. ⓐ Langestraat 69 ⓣ 0473 73 34 60 ⓛ 17.00–late

ⓞ *The gracious city of Ghent*

OUT OF TOWN
trips

Damme

The picturesque little village of Damme is, believe it or not, officially a city. Its status and former wealth derives from the fact that it was once the landing stage where large vessels off-loaded their cargo to smaller ships or barges to be landed in Bruges. It was so important – before the Zwin estuary finally silted up and both Bruges and Damme became backwaters – that Charles the Bold, the last Duke of Burgundy and ruler of Flanders, married Margaret of York, sister of Edward IV of England, in the city in 1468. It was earlier the site of a dyke or dam (hence the name) on the Zwin creek. At its height, more than 300 types of goods landed there, and the city had the right to import Bordeaux wine and Swedish herrings. You can still visit the 15th-century herring market.

Now the centre of an agricultural area, it's the perfect day-trip destination from Bruges, and welcomes 100,000 visitors a year. This explains why 25 restaurants, many of them very good, serve this village with a resident population of 700, though around 11,000 people live in the surrounding area.

Tourist Office ⊙ Jacob van Maerlanstraat 3, on the main square, in one of Damme's grandest houses ⊙ 050 28 86 10
ⓦ www.vvvdamme.be ⊙ 09.00–12.00 & 14.00–18.00 Mon–Fri, 10.00–12.00 & 14.00–18.00 Sat & Sun (16 Apr–15 Oct); 09.00–12.00 & 14.00–17.00 Mon–Fri, 14.00–17.00 Sat & Sun (16 Oct–15 Apr)

GETTING THERE

Damme is only 7 km (4½ miles) from Bruges, and there are several ways of getting there. The most straightforward is simply to walk along the Bruges-Damme Canal, which starts at the Damport gate to the northwest of Bruges' city centre, near the northernmost

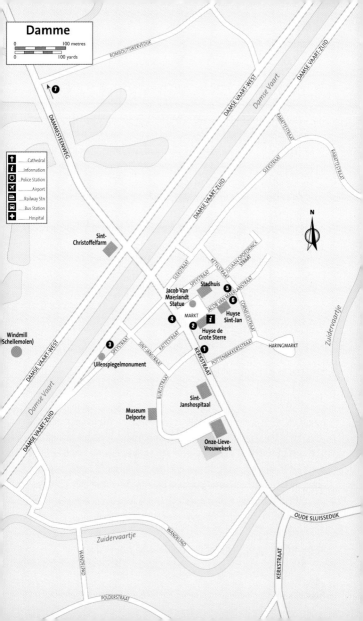

Damme

| 0 | 100 metres |
| 0 | 100 yards |

✝	Cathedral
𝒊	Information
⊙	Police Station
✈	Airport
▭	Railway Stn
⊟	Bus Station
✚	Hospital

ROMBOUTSWERVEDIJK

DAMSE VAART-WEST

Damse Vaart

DAMSE VAART-ZUID

DAMMESTENWEG

SLEKSTRAAT

RABATSTRAAT

N

Sint-Christoffelfarm

Windmill (Schellemolen)

DAMSE VAART-WEST

DAMSE VAART-ZUID

Damse Vaart

SLEKSTRAAT

SPEISTRAAT

KETELSTRAAT

LIUAN OPSDRINCK STRAAT

Stadhuis

Jacob Van Maerlandt Statue

JACOB VAN MAERLANTSTRAAT

CORNELISSTRAAT

❺

❻

Huyse Sint-Jan

MARKT

❹

❷

𝒊

Huyse de Grote Sterre

❶

HARINGMARKT

SPEISTRAAT

❸

Uilenspiegelmonument

SINT-JANSTRAAT

KATTESTRAAT

KERKSTRAAT

POTTENBAKKERSSTRAAT

Zuidervaartje

BURGSTRAAT

Museum Delporte

Sint-Janshospitaal

Onze-Lieve-Vrouwekerk

OUDE SLUISEDIJK

Zuidervaartje

WANDELPAD

WANDELPAD

POLDERSTRAAT

KERKSTRAAT

❼

windmill on the Kruisvest. There is also a bicycle path along the canal, and you can take a guided ride from Bruges, which also covers the countryside around Damme (www.quasimundo.com).

If you feel too full of beer and chocolate to face such energetic activity, you can also drive along the road running parallel to the Bruges-Damme Canal and you'll be at your destination in about 10–15 minutes. A taxi will cost you around €25. If you want a cheaper option, take a bus from either Markt or the railway station (No. 43). They leave every two hours, more frequently in the afternoon. The last return bus from Damme leaves at 17.55. Buses run from Easter to September, except during school holidays.

You can also take minibus tours from Markt or canal-boat excursions. A one-way canal trip lasts 35 minutes. The departure point in Bruges is Noorweegse Kaai 31 (No. 4 bus from Markt). Boats leave every two hours, on the hour, from 10.00. The last boat back from Damme leaves at 17.20. Tickets from Bruges cost €6.70 return (€5.20 one-way). Canal-boat trips run from April to 15 October.

SIGHTS & ATTRACTIONS

Apart from wandering round, eating and drinking, and generally hanging out in a very pretty place, not even the most fervent local resident could claim that Damme has any major must-see attractions. The best of the buildings is generally to be seen from the outside. But don't let that put you off; it's a very refreshing place, though in high season there will be several hundred other tourists there. There's also a windmill, the canal and some small shops to go to. And the countryside around, including villages such as Oosterkerke,

● *The attractive clock tower of the Stadhuis dates back to 1459*

Vivenkapelle, Moerkerke and Lapscheure – near the border with the Netherlands – are also pleasant if you are travelling by car or bike. You can get a real feel for the Flemish countryside there. But you'll probably spend most of your time in Damme in or near the main square.

CULTURE

Onze-Lieve-Vrouwekerk (Church of Our Lady)

The oldest part of this imposing Gothic edifice – between the tower and the church – was erected in 1225. The church itself dates from the 14th century, when Damme's population increased, but was forcibly modified in the 18th century, when the original nave, the aisles and the transept partly collapsed, and the locals couldn't afford to restore it, so diminished was Damme's wealth by then. The tower is 43 m (141 ft) high, and you can get very good views of Damme and the surrounding countryside if you're willing to hike to the top.
ⓐ Kerkstraat ⓦ www.damme-online.com ⓛ 10.30–12.00 & 14.30–17.30 Easter & May–Sept; tiny admission charge each for church and tower

Schellemolen (windmill)

You can visit Damme's nearest windmill, built in 1867 on the site of others going back to the Middle Ages.
ⓐ Damse Vaart West ⓦ www.damme-online.com ⓛ 09.30–12.30 & 13.00–18.00 Sat, Sun & public holidays (summer), or with a guide at other times; free admission

Sint-Janshospitaal

Dating from 1249, the complex is still an old people's home and hospital. The building itself is worth looking at; and it has a museum of religious objects, ceramics, furniture and some paintings, which is somewhat less enticing, but not uninteresting. The chapel is largely baroque.

🅐 Kerkstraat 33 Ⓦ www.ocmw-damme.be ⏱ museum 14.00–18.00 Mon & Fri, 11.00–12.00 & 14.00–18.00 Tues–Thur, Sat & Sun (Easter–Sept); 14.00–16.30 (Oct–Easter); small admission charge

Stadhuis (City Hall)

You can't enter it (except by arrangement at the Tourist Office), but this notable Gothic building on the main square, with its sturdy and heavily augmented façade, was originally built in 1464, and is on the site of the old market hall. The exterior was restored in the 19th

⬤ Sint-Janshospitaal is still a home for the elderly, but also a museum

century. Two of the stone figures on the façade (on the far right, as you look at it) are of Charles the Bold and Margaret of York. The clock tower, which dominates the village, dates from 1459. In front of the Stadhuis is a 19th-century statue of Jacob van Maerlant (1235–93), a Flemish poet and Damme resident.

ⓐ Marktplein ⓦ www.damme-online.com

RETAIL THERAPY

There are the usual souvenir shops in Damme, but very few others, except for those serving the daily needs of the local population. However, since 1997 Damme has tried to establish itself as a book town (rather like Hay-on-Wye in Wales, but on a much smaller scale). As a result, ten bookshops have been attracted to the village. Most of them sell second-hand books, some of them in English. The shops are open daily May–Sept, but only at weekends the rest of the year. There is a book market in the main square during the second Sunday of every month, which transfers to the City Hall in winter. If you do want souvenirs, the following is worth a try:

Tijl en Nele A small souvenir shop selling local specialities, including beer. You can also get a sandwich there. ⓐ Jacob van Maerlantstraat 2 ⓛ closed Fri (summer); closed Wed, Thur & Fri (winter)

TAKING A BREAK

Tante Marie £ ❶ A bright, modern tea room serving salads and other snacks, high-quality patisserie and ice cream. You can also take food away. ⓐ Kerkstraat 38 ⓛ 10.00–19.00, closed Fri

Eetcafé de Spieghel £–££ ❷ A brasserie on the main square in a 16th-century merchant's house, with a rustic interior where you can get a full lunch, or a snack from 15.00 to 18.00 in summer. It has tables outside. ⓐ Jacob van Maerlantstraat 1 🕐 11.30–24.00, kitchen closes at 22.00, closed Tues (summer); 11.30–15.00 & 18.00–22.00, closed Mon & Tues (winter)

⬤ The market square viewed from the top of the Gothic Stadhuis (City Hall)

Hotel de Speye £–££ ❸ On a canal. Best for a snack (omelette, sandwich or crêpe, for instance) or a drink, rather than a full meal. ⓐ Damse Vaart-Zuid 5–6 🕐 11.00–21.00, closed Mon

AFTER DARK

Restaurants
De Drie Zilveren Kannen ££ ❹ In a 15th-century gabled house, with mullioned windows, on the main square. Smart décor, candle-lit in

▲ *Wine and dine in traditional splendour*

the evening. Gastronomic food, highly rated locally. 🅐 Markt 9
🅕 050 35 56 77 🅛 11.30–15.00 & 17.30–22.00, closed Mon

De Lieve ££ ❺ One of Damme's oldest restaurants, decorated in
country style, serving high-quality gastronomic food – light and
pleasingly presented – and excellent wines. 🅐 Jacob van
Maerlantstraat 10 🅕 050 35 66 30 🅛 closed Mon evening & Tues

Eethuis de Zuidkant ££ ❻ Recently renovated, mixing modern and
traditional décor (with an open kitchen). Contemporary food in a
relaxed atmosphere which attracts many of Flanders' top chefs, as
well as the public. 🅐 Jacob van Maerlantstraat 6 🅕 050 37 16 76
🅛 12.00–14.00 & 19.00–21.00, closed Wed & Thur

Siphon ££ A little way out of town, with large picture windows
looking out on to the countryside. One of the best-known
restaurants in the country, serving Belgian food, and game in
season. The atmosphere is relaxed, and the place is normally so
popular with families that there are two sittings for lunch (12.00
and 13.00) and dinner (18.00 and 20.00). You can't book other times.
🅐 Oostkerke
🅕 050 62 02 02 🅛 closed Thur, Fri, Feb & Oct

Bars
S…Misse A lively bar/café with a mostly young crowd and good
background music. A wide selection of beers and an outside terrace.
🅐 Kerkstraat 6 🅛 open until late, closed Mon

Ghent

Ghent (Gent in Flemish, Gand in French) is superficially similar to Bruges, but different in many ways. It is bigger and architecturally much less coherent. It also has several local heavy industries, such as car production, and is a vibrant university town, with many more young people. It is much more 'real', and less touristy than Bruges, but with its fair share of major attractions. In other words, it's a significant city first and a tourist destination second.

On the junction of two rivers – the Leie (Lys) and the Scheldt (Schelde) – Ghent is an important port, one of the oldest cities in Flanders, and now capital of the East Flanders province. Its history is similar to that of Bruges; once highly important in textile production and extremely prosperous as a result, but declining in the 16th century. Unlike Bruges, however, Ghent embraced the Industrial Revolution in the 19th century, and its fortunes revived as a result.

Tourist Office In the crypt of the Belfort. There are also public toilets there. ⓐ Botermarkt 17a ⓣ 09 266 52 32 ⓦ www.visitgent.be ⓛ 09.30–18.30 (summer); 09.30–16.30 (winter)

GETTING THERE

Ghent is only 40 km (25 miles) from Bruges, and easy to drive to via the E40, but parking can be a problem. A much better option is to take the train to Gent Sint-Pieters station. Trains to and from Bruges are frequent (around every half-hour), comfortable, quick (20–25 minutes) and cheap (€10.40 return). Then you can either take a taxi into the centre or tram 1 to Korenmarkt, from the platform just to the left of the train station as you come out of the main entrance. It takes 15 minutes. The tram's stops are shown on an on-board display.

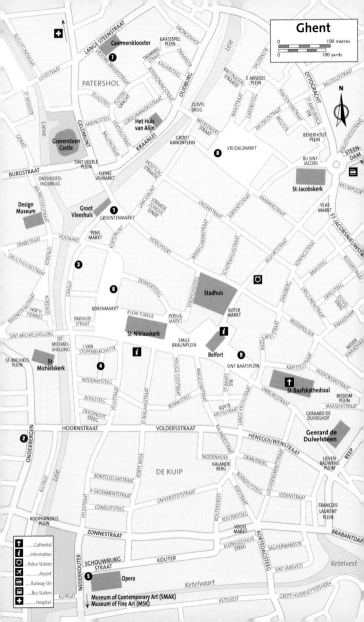

SIGHTS & ATTRACTIONS

All the sights you might be tempted to see are within easy walking distance in the city centre. There is no real hub to the centre, but several squares (**Korenmarkt**, **Sint-Baafsplein**, **Groentenmarkt** and **Vrijdagmarkt**) are near, and linked to each other. Many of the streets are pedestrianised, and even more are cobbled, so wear comfortable shoes. If you can identify the **Belfort**, and the spires of **Sint-Baafskathedraal** and **Sint-Niklaaskerk**, you shouldn't get lost. As in Bruges, many people speak English and will help you with directions.

One of the striking things about Ghent and, on the whole, a contrast to Bruges, is the number of buildings which have old façades but ultra-modern interiors. Indeed, some impressive-looking old buildings retain only their façades and are completely rebuilt, modern structures behind. You will see this mixture of old and contemporary architecture in many restaurants, hotels and, appropriately, in the **Design Museum**.

Apart from visiting the main buildings and museums, you are also likely to be tempted to sit in a canalside or riverside café, or simply to picnic by some water. You can also take canal-boat trips, and horse-drawn carriage rides which set off from Sint-Baafsplein (€25 for a 30-minute ride in a carriage that seats up to five). Guided boat trips last from 40 to 90 minutes (€5 to €9). Canal boats go from Kraanlei, Korenlei, Graslei and Groentenmarkt bridge, and there are several good shops selling local produce to pop into.

Ghent also hosts several festivals, particularly in the summer. Perhaps the most fun is the **Ghent Festivities** (De Gentse Feesten): ten days of entertainment starting in the third week of July. Ghent Festivities is actually four festivals at once: a jazz festival, a dance festival (with the latest dances), a street-theatre festival and a puppet festival. During the Festivities, there are plenty of open-air and free music events (www.gentsefeesten.be). There is also a film festival in October.

Ghent boasts several concert halls, theatres, art centres, cinemas and an opera house (with a resident company). Much of the centre of Ghent is floodlit at night, and the city has a dynamic nightlife (quite unlike Bruges), though some of the hippest places for music and dancing are a distance from the centre.

⬤ *The Design Museum's exhibits include Art Nouveau and Art Deco pieces*

Incidentally, if you have to wait for a train, the **Miljoenenkwartier** area behind the station has a number of Art Nouveau and Art Deco buildings worth looking at.

CULTURE

There are numerous museums, churches and monuments in Ghent, of varying degrees of interest. Some of the museums – including a psychiatric hospital and one about the textile industry – are for those with a lot of time to kill, but below are the sights you might want to visit on a short trip. You can buy a pass (€12.50) from the main museums, the tourist office and some hotels, which will take you into most of the main attractions.

Belfort

The 91-m (298-ft) belfry dominates Ghent, and can be seen from around the city. It is topped by a gilded copper dragon weathervane. It was once the city's watchtower: the bells were used to warn the citizens of danger from enemies and to announce major events. Construction started in early 1314, but the tower has had many makeovers through the years, particularly in the 19th century. The current dragon dates from just 1980. The Belfort is arranged on six floors, with a small museum on the first and second, the bells on the third, the mechanism of the clock on the fifth, and excellent views of the city from the sixth. You can take a lift to the fourth floor. You'll find the tourist office in the basement of the building.
ⓐ Emile Brauplein ⏰ 10.00–12.30, 14.00–17.30; small admission charge

ⓞ *The Belfort was once Ghent's watchtower*

Design Museum

Definitely worth visiting, this is a superb museum, opened in 1992 in the 18th-century Hotel de Coninck. But appearances are deceptive. Although older furniture and other artefacts are housed in traditionally decorated rooms at the front of the building, the heart of the museum is firmly contemporary, consisting of a bold, bright series of spaces displaying exhibits from the Art Nouveau and Art Deco periods to the most recent of objects by designers such as Phillipe Starck, Ron Arad and Jean Nouvel. There are also regular temporary exhibitions.

ⓐ Jan Breydelstraat 5 ☏ 09 267 99 99
ⓦ www.design.museum.gent.be ◷ 10.00–18.00, closed Mon; small admission charge

Gravensteen (Castle of the Counts)

Built in 1180 by Philip of Alsace, Count of Flanders, this is an imposing, if not particularly attractive, edifice. Like much else in Ghent, the castle has been heavily restored and it is undergoing more work at the time of writing. There are displays of weapons and other artefacts, and those with a penchant for the dark and terrible will be attracted to the small museum of instruments of torture. You can also see the dungeons. If you climb to the battlements, you will get some worthwhile views of the city.

ⓐ Sint-Veerleplein ☏ 09 225 93 06 ⓦ www.gent.be ◷ 09.00–18.00 (summer); 09.00–17.00 (winter); admission charge

Museum voor Schone Kunsten/MSK (Museum of Fine Arts)

Going for over a century, the MSK is being renovated at the time of writing and is due to re-open in 2007. This museum has one of the finest collections in Belgium, which originated with acquisitions in the 18th century from old churches and other religious institutions. Exhibits range from medieval Flemish paintings to mid-20th-century works. Big names on display include Bruegel, Hals, Tintoretto, Rubens, Renoir, van Dyck and Kokoschka. The museum also mounts special exhibitions from time to time (usually at extra cost). During the restoration, some of its works have been dispersed to other locations in Ghent (including the crypt of Sint-Baafskathedraal). These will return when work on the museum is finished.

@ Citadelpark ⓦ www.mskgent.be 🕐 10.00–18.00, closed Mon; small admission charge

Sint-Baafskathedraal

Founded before the 10th century, this was the first parish church in Ghent, known as St John's until the 16th century, and was substantially enlarged during those 600 years. It became a cathedral in 1561, named after St Bavo, the local 7th-century saint. Its architecture is largely Gothic, but the pulpit is rococo. There are no fewer than 22 chapels in the building (which isn't particularly inspiring from the outside), and many works of art dotted about the place, including Rubens' *The Conversion of St Bavo*. The 12th-century Romanesque crypt – one of the biggest in Belgium – is the oldest existing part, and also contains several fine Flemish paintings, including works by Hieronymus Bosch. Some of these paintings, including those by Bosch, will return to the Museum of Fine Arts after its renovation is completed (see below).

There aren't many individual works of art in the world that can, by themselves, attract visitors to a city, but Jan and Hubert van Eyck's *Adoration of the Mystic Lamb* (also known as 'The Ghent Altarpiece') certainly does. This stunning work, finished in 1432 – and much bigger than you might expect – is in a chapel to the left as

you enter. Despite the crowds in the cramped chapel in high season, you really shouldn't miss it. Note particularly the rich colours and the remarkable use of light and landscape. Such is the reputation of the work that it has been looted several times – by the Nazis on the last occasion – and finally returned to the cathedral after World War II. One panel, stolen in 1934, is still missing. Note that entry times for the chapel aren't the same as for the cathedral.

ⓐ Sint-Baafsplein **ⓣ** 09 225 16 26 **ⓦ** www.sintbaafskathedraal-gent.be **ⓛ** cathedral 08.30–18.00 (summer); 08.30–17.00 (winter); closed during services, including Sun morning and religious holidays; *Adoration of the Mystic Lamb* 09.30–16.30 Mon–Sat, 13.00–16.30 Sun (summer); 10.30–15.30 Mon–Sat, 13.00–15.30 Sun (winter); small admission charge

Stedelijk Museum voor Actuele Kunst/SMAK (Municipal Museum of Contemporary Art)

Near the MSK, and opened in 1975, this is recognised as the finest modern-art museum in Belgium, with over 1,500 paintings and sculptures, including works by David Hockney, Francis Bacon and Andy Warhol, as well as Belgian artists such as Magritte. Major special exhibitions are displayed on the ground floor.

ⓐ Citadelpark **ⓦ** www.smak.be **ⓛ** 10.00–18.00, closed Mon; admission charge

RETAIL THERAPY

The main shopping street in Ghent is Veldstraat, south of Korenmarkt. The area around it is also full of smart shops, including international chains. The other good street for shops is Langemunt, just off Groentenmarkt. Go to Burgstraat for antiques and bric-a-brac, and

Hoogpoort and Bennesteeg for fashion and accessories. You will see plenty of small boutiques, food and speciality shops scattered around the old city. Many smaller shops don't take credit cards.

Markets you might want to visit include one selling the colourful flowers Ghent is famous for (ⓐ Kouter ⓛ 07.00–13.00 Mon–Sun), a flea market (ⓐ Bij Sint-Jacobs ⓛ 08.00–13.00 Sat & Sun) and food market (ⓐ St-Michielsplein ⓛ 07.30–13.00 Sun). There is also a market selling new goods of various types (ⓐ Vrijdagmarkt ⓛ Fri & Sat), and, if you like feathery friends, a bird market (ⓐ Vrijdagmarkt ⓛ Sun morning).

Some of Ghent's more intriguing shops are:

Caron Selling pens, cigars, desk accessories and other stylish boys' toys. ⓐ Veldstraat 45 ⓣ 09 225 35 44

Het Oorcussen One of the best women's clothes shops in town, featuring leading Belgian designers, in a 16th-century building. ⓐ Vrijdagmarkt 7 ⓣ 09 233 07 65

Temmerman A charmingly old-fashioned confectionery shop selling sweets, chocolates and biscuits, including the local speciality, *cuberdon* (conical sweets made from raspberry syrup and gum arabic). ⓐ Kraanlei 79 ⓣ 09 224 00 41

The Fallen Angels Thoroughly eccentric, selling old toys, religious memorabilia, bric-a-brac, old postcards and anything else that takes the fancy of the mother and daughter running these two shops. ⓐ Jan Breydelstraat 29–31 ⓣ 09 223 94 15

Tierenteyn Dating from 1858 (and a listed building), this beautiful shop sells hot home-made, preservative-free mustard, and a good

selection of herbs, spices, oils and vinegars. The lovely interior with its old ceramic jars is worth a visit in itself. ⓐ Groentenmarkt 3 ⓘ 09 225 83 36

TAKING A BREAK

There are any number of cafés, bars and restaurants around the centre of Ghent, some very stylish, and delicatessens (or the markets mentioned above) are great places to buy picnic supplies for that relaxing loll by a canal or in the leafy Citadelpark. Many of the cafés are by the waterside, and there are relatively few tourist traps. There is also a popular chip kiosk in Vrijdagmarkt. The following is a particularly pleasant spot to take a break in:

Groot Vleeshuis £ ❶ Opened in 2002 on the former site of the covered 15th-century meat market, this is both a restaurant and a delicatessen firmly devoted to East Flemish produce, including ham, mustard, beer, chocolate and *jenever* (gin). You can eat inside or out. Great for snacks or a light meal. ⓐ Groentenmarkt 7 ⓘ 09 223 23 24 ⓛ 10.00–18.00

AFTER DARK

Restaurants

As a rule, restaurants and cafés are somewhat cheaper than they are in Bruges, and often open later. Apart from the places mentioned below, Ghent also has many non-Belgian restaurants (Thai, Greek, Italian and Indian, for instance).

◀ *The waterfront is good for a stroll and a coffee*

De Kastart £ ❷ A cheap and cheerful place, popular with students, famous for its spaghetti. ⓐ Onderbergen 42 ❶ 09 224 36 27 ❸ 11.30–23.30

Belga Queen £–££ ❸ One of Belgium's most famous brasseries, serving top quality food in an impressively modern conversion of a 13th-century grain storehouse by the Leie river, with tables outside in good weather. There is also a bar and a cigar lounge. The place is a tea room in the afternoon. The set lunch menu is a bargain. ⓐ Graslei 10 ❶ 09 280 01 00 ⓦ www.belgaqueen.be ❸ 12.00–14.30 & 19.00–24.00

Brasserie Pakhuis £–££ ❹ One of the most fashionable places in Ghent, in an old warehouse. French and Italian food, and excellent seafood. A bar and tea room throughout the day. Surprisingly reasonable set menus, particularly at lunch. ⓐ Schuurkenstraat 4 ❶ 09 223 55 55 ❸ 11.30–01.00 Sun–Thur, 11.30–02.00 Fri & Sat

Café Théâtre £–££ ❺ A modern, split-level bar with dark brown walls and relaxed atmosphere, and a restaurant. Next to the opera house. You can get a snack in the bar, or a fuller (more expensive) meal in the restaurant. ⓐ Schouwburgstraat 5 ❶ 09 265 05 50 ❸ restaurant 12.00–14.15 & 19.00–23.00; bar 10.00–late

Du Progrès £–££ ❻ Very popular with locals. No-nonsense food and quick service. ⓐ Korenmarkt 10 ❶ 09 225 17 16

Karel de Stoute £–££ ❼ Good, traditional food. ⓐ Vrouwebroersstraat 5–7 ❶ 09 224 17 35

Keizershof £–££ ❶ Going strong for over 25 years. You can get salads, pasta or more substantial Belgian dishes, all in a handsomely restored building. ⓐ Vrijdagmarkt 47 ❶ 09 223 44 46 ⓛ 12.00–14.00 & 18.00–22.00

't Vosken £–££ ❾ A traditional brasserie close to Sint-Baafskathedraal. Popular and reasonable value. ⓐ St-Baafsplein 19 ❶ 09 225 73 61 ⓛ until 24.00

Bars

Dulle Griet An atmospheric beer bar (250 types on offer) where you can also get light nibbles. ⓐ Vrijdagmarkt 50 ❶ 09 224 24 55 ⓛ 12.30–01.00, closed Sun evening

Igor New bar, with a café serving pasta, salads and tapas. Varnished wood walls, floor and seating. Situated in a student area, it stays open beyond its usual hours on weekends. ⓐ Grote Huidevettershoek 10 ❶ 09 224 36 93 ⓛ 11.00–01.30

ACCOMMODATION

Ghent has accommodation to suit all pockets, and it's usually cheaper than equivalent places in Bruges. There are few really smart hotels in town, but at the time of writing a new Marriott hotel is being built on the banks of the Leie. Remember that hotels will be much fuller during events such as the Ghent Festivities. Below is a small selection. The best place to get detailed information is www.visitgent.be

Ibis Gent Centrum Opera £ Part of a chain, with pleasant rooms and good value. ⓐ Nederkouter 24–26 ⓣ 09 225 07 07 ⓦ www.ibishotel.com

Monasterium £ Simple, brightly decorated rooms in an old monastery. The hotel's guesthouse has cheaper rooms, but you will have to share a bathroom. ⓐ Oude Houtlei 56 ⓣ 09 269 22 10 ⓦ www.monasterium.be

Ghent River Hotel ££ With a modern frontage (and interiors), but developed from two old buildings on the Leie river. ⓐ Waaistraat 5 ⓣ 09 266 10 10 ⓦ www.ghent-river-hotel.be

Hotel de Flandre ££ A stylish, very comfortable hotel converted from a 19th-century inn (a listed building). ⓐ Poel 1–2 ⓣ 09 266 06 00 ⓦ www.hoteldeflandre.be

Hotel Harmony ££ Modern décor in a converted 18th-century warehouse. ⓐ Kraanlei 37 ⓣ 09 324 26 80 ⓦ www.hotelharmony.be

Hotel Verhaegen ££ Only four rooms in an old mansion, but one of the most stylish addresses in town; as it should be: it is owned by two interior designers. It's really a B&B, but that title doesn't begin to do the place justice. ⓐ Oude Houtlei 110 ⓣ 09 265 07 65 ⓦ www.hotelverhaegen.be

Sofitel Gent Belfort ££–£££ Smart and comfortable with excellent facilities. ⓐ Hoogpoort 63 ⓣ 09 233 33 31 ⓦ www.sofitel.com

● *The imposing Gravensteen has been heavily restored*

Ypres & World War I Battlefields

Ypres (Ieper) is about as friendly to British, Commonwealth and American visitors as it is possible to be. It not only relies on their tourism for its economy, but there are also many links between local organisations and those in Britain and the Commonwealth. The reason isn't difficult to fathom. The area around Ypres (or 'Wipers' as British Tommies called it) was the site of many of World War I's bloodiest battles, including Paschendale. Some 500,000 soldiers lost their lives around Ypres, half of them from Britain and the Commonwealth, and many more thousands returned home wounded. The battles were also fought by Belgian, French and, later, American soldiers. Their graves surround the town (there are over 170 cemeteries), and the Menin Gate and the In Flanders Fields Museum in Ypres commemorate their sacrifice. Ypres and the surrounding area was also devastated by shelling in World War I, so there is a strong bond. As a result, English is not only spoken everywhere, but there are also signs and shop names in English.

Like Bruges, Ypres grew quickly in the 12th century because of the cloth trade, and had 40,000 inhabitants by 1260. As a result, there is still a certain grandeur in its public buildings, particularly in the main square. It suffered a sharp economic decline in the 14th century, and was then little heard of until 1914 and World War I. It took over 40 years to rebuild the town after its destruction. Tourism apart, Ypres is now rather a quiet, charming town. You don't come here for the boisterous nightlife; most places are closed by 23.00.

Most visitors – many of them descendants of those who fought or died here – come to see the battlefields and war graves, learn about World War I, and remember those who died. These include

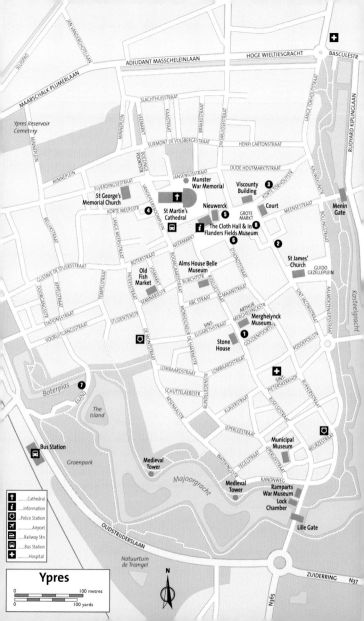

Ypres

0 _____ 100 metres
0 _____ 100 yards

British children on school trips. As a result, Ypres' inhabitants expect a certain amount of decorum from visitors. The town is overwhelmed by British tourists on 11 November, Remembrance Day.

Tourist Office The office also has a stylish shop selling books, postcards and souvenirs. ⓐ Cloth Hall, Grote Markt 34 ⓣ 057 23 92 20 ⓦ www.ieper.be ⓛ 09.00–18.00 Mon–Sat, 10.00–18.00 Sun & public holidays (1 Apr–30 Sept); 09.00–17.00 Mon–Fri, 10.00–17.00 Sat, Sun & holidays, closed Christmas Day and New Year's Day (1 Oct–31 Mar)

GETTING THERE

You can go by train to Ypres from Bruges via Kortrijk. This can take up to two hours. The station is a ten-minute walk from the centre of town. Driving will take you an hour or more on the A17, E403 and A19. On arrival, you can park in the market square (but not on Saturday, when there is a market) or behind the Cloth Hall. All-inclusive, full-day coach tours of Ypres and the Flanders battlefields, with lunch, drinks and museum entry, leave from Bruges and cost €59 per adult. They run every day from February to December, except on Mondays and Tuesdays. Quasimodo (www.quasimodo.be) offers one of the best and most relaxed minibus tours.

SIGHTS & ATTRACTIONS

Battlefield visits

If you make your own way to Ypres, you can visit the battlefields yourself; there are battlefield route maps for both drivers and cyclists available from the tourist office. Bicycles can be hired from Ypres railway station. Alternatively, you can join one of the many

ⓞ *Remembering those who died in World War I at Ypres*

local battlefield tours, some of which are given by private guides who will take you around in a car. The cemetery at Paschendale (Passendale) is particularly moving, and the German war cemetery, at Langemark – where 48,000 German soldiers are buried – is also worth visiting, though it is very different in design and atmosphere from the British cemeteries. Among the best local tours are those organised by the following:

Flanders Battlefield Tour ❶ 057 36 04 60 ⓦ www.ypres-fbt.be

R J Motor-Bikertours ❶ 0494 12 60 34 ❷ rjmotorbikes@hotmail.com

Salient Tours ❶ 057 36 04 60 ⓦ www.salienttours.com

Speedy's Battlefield Tours Run by an exuberant and knowledgeable local taxi driver nicknamed Speedy, who can also take you back to Bruges. ❶ 0478 32 99 29 ⓦ www.sbt-ypers.be

Grote Markt (Main Square)

The main square is an attraction in its own right, featuring the **Cloth Hall**, dating from the 13th century, and once the biggest non-religious building in Europe. The hall was almost completely destroyed during World War I, but was slowly rebuilt over the following decades. It houses the **In Flanders Fields Museum** on the first floor (see 'Culture' page 136). The **Nieuwerck** (Town Hall) is next to the Cloth Hall. Originally built in 1619, it was rebuilt in 1962. You can visit the grand council chamber here if you feel the need to be indoors for a bit (08.30–11.45 Mon–Fri). The **Kasselrij** building, in the middle of the main square, was previously used as the town hall. Check out the beautifully carved medallions above the ground-floor windows representing the Seven Deadly Sins.

◀ *The 13th-century Cloth Hall at Ypres*

Just behind the Cloth Hall is the Gothic **St Martin's Cathedral**, again completely rebuilt after World War I. Nearby is **St George's Memorial Church**, an Anglican church built in 1928 to commemorate the war dead.

Menin Gate

One of Ypres' most impressive sights is the Menin Gate, by the city's ramparts, designed by Sir Reginald Blomfield (also the architect of St George's Memorial Church). This poignant and very dignified memorial has the names of almost 55,000 missing British and Commonwealth soldiers engraved on its walls. The Last Post is sounded every evening at 20.00.

CULTURE

In Flanders Fields Museum

This is a superb, modern museum which brilliantly evokes the atmosphere and history of World War I, using the latest interactive techniques and moving displays. Last admission to the museum is an hour before closing time.

ⓐ Cloth Hall, Grote Markt ① 057 23 92 20 ⓦ www.inflandersfields.be
ⓛ 10.00–18.00, closed Mon (Apr–Sept); 10.00–17.00, closed Mon (Oct–Mar); admission charged

RETAIL THERAPY

Ypres is no retail mecca, but in this little centre you'll find the usual tourist-oriented chocolate, beer and lace shops,

---

◗ *One of the atmospheric displays at the In Flanders Field Museum*

as well as bookshops catering to those with an interest in World War I.

TAKING A BREAK

There are several decent cafés and bars, all near Grote Markt and the Menin Gate, with prices somewhat lower than they are in Bruges. Among the best are:

Het Zilveren Hoofd £ **❶** **ⓐ** Rijselsestraat 49 **❶** 057 21 73 78

Old Bill £ **❷** **ⓐ** Sint-Jacobsstraat 10 **❶** 0477 28 49 37

The Times £ **❸** **ⓐ** Korte Torhoutstraat 7 **❶** 057 20 99 30

't Leetvermaak £ **❹** **ⓐ** Korte Meersstraat 2 **❶** 057 21 63 85

AFTER DARK

Restaurants
You can eat well in Ypres. Among the better restaurants are:

In 't Klein Stadhuis £ **❺** The name means 'Little Town Hall', and it's right next door to the real one. An inviting and friendly place, with a bar and decent food in a warm atmosphere. The salads come in very large portions. **ⓐ** Grote Markt 32 **❶** 057 21 55 42

◀ *The names of at least 55,000 missing soldiers are engraved on the Menin Gate*

Old Tom ££ ❻ There's a cosy atmosphere in this hotel, specialising in fish and seafood as well as game. ⓐ Grote Markt 8 ❶ 057 20 15 41

Pacific Eiland ££ ❼ Regional food by the ramparts and the water. Also has a bistro and tea room, and a terrace in the summer. ⓐ Eiland 2 ❶ 057 20 05 28

Regina ££ ❽ A hotel restaurant with a warm welcome and high-quality cooking. ⓐ Grote Markt 45 ❶ 057 21 88 88

ACCOMMODATION

Flanders Lodge £ A wooden building offering a warm atmosphere. ⓐ Dehemlaan 19 ❶ 057 21 70 00

The Shell Hole £ A small family hotel, with a World War I bookshop, in the town centre. English breakfast is included. ⓐ D' Hondtstraat 54 ❶ 057 20 87 58

Ariane ££ A good-quality, modern hotel with friendly staff, five minutes' walk from Grote Martk. ⓐ Slachthuisstraat 58 ❶ 057 21 82 18 ⓦ www.ariane.be

❶ *Bruges' City Theatre*

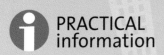

PRACTICAL
information

Directory

GETTING THERE

By air

Brussels Zaventem is a major airport, and British Airways, Lufthansa and bmi all fly the one-hour journey there from Britain, as do other major airlines from most of the world's main cities. All three take off from Heathrow, but British Airways has flights from other airports, too, and bmi also flies from Nottingham. Aer Lingus flies from Dublin. In addition, Ryanair flies to Charleroi (an hour away from Brussels) from Stansted. Fares on all these carriers vary depending on the season, day of the week and, primarily, how far in advance you book. Flights from other countries include Delta, American Airlines and British Airways from New York; and Air Canada, Delta, British Airways and Lufthansa from Toronto.

Aer Lingus Ⓦ www.aerlingus.ie

bmi Ⓦ www.flybmi.com

British Airways Ⓦ www.ba.com

Ryanair Ⓦ www.ryanair.com

Many people are aware that air travel emits CO_2, which contributes to climate change. You may be interested in the possibility of lessening the environmental impact of your flight through the charity Climate Care, which offsets your CO_2 by funding environmental projects around the world. Visit www.climatecare.org for details.

By train

Travelling to Brussels by Eurostar from London Waterloo at the time of writing (soon to be St Pancras) or Ashford International is probably the most relaxing way to travel. It takes around 3½ hours to get to Bruges. There are up to ten daily services, and prices compare very well with all but the cheapest low-cost air fares. Local trains depart regularly for Bruges from the same Brussels station (Midi/Zuid) as the Eurostar arrives at, and take 50–60 minutes to get to Bruges. A great advantage is that your Eurostar ticket entitles you to travel on these trains (or to any other Belgian station on the same day) at no extra cost. The same applies on the day of your return Eurostar journey. Fares on the Eurostar start at £59 return in standard class. They can be more expensive, depending on the time of day you travel, and how far in advance you book. Don't forget that you need to allow at least 30 minutes to check in, on departure from

◆ Hop on and sit back for a tour of the city's delights

both London and Brussels. An alternative is to take the Eurostar to Lille Europe Station, and then walk to Lille Flandres Station and take a local train to Bruges; it may be quicker, but not necessarily so.

Eurostar reservations ☎ 0870 5186 186 (UK) ⓦ www.eurostar.com

By car

If you decide to travel by car from the UK, there are several ways of getting to Belgium. Depending on where you live, you can take ferries to Calais (from Dover), Ostend (from Ramsgate) and Zeebrugge (from Hull and Rosyth); or you can go by Eurotunnel (35 minutes to cross the Channel to France). You eventually need to get on the E40/A10 to get to Bruges from Calais (around 90 minutes), or Ostend (30 minutes). From Zeebrugge, you take the N31 (less than 30 minutes). The city centre of Bruges is encircled by a ring road.

ⓘ Remember that you will scarcely use your car in Bruges itself, and might have problems parking, though some hotels have their own car parks.

Eurotunnel ⓦ www.eurotunnel.com
P&O Ferries (Dover, Hull) ⓦ www.poferries.com

TRAVEL INSURANCE

Visitors from the UK are covered by EU reciprocal health schemes while in Belgium. They require a European Health Insurance Card (EHIC). Remember that this will not cover all possible expenses, and only guarantees emergency treatment. Whether an EU or a non-EU traveller, always make sure you have adequate travel insurance, covering not only health, but possessions, etc.

Superfast Ferries (Rosyth) ⓦ www.superfast.com
Transeuropa Ferries (Ramsgate) ⓦ www.transeuropaferries.com

ENTRY FORMALITIES
Documentation
Passports are needed by UK visitors and all others except EU citizens who can produce a national identity card. Visits of up to three months do not require a visa if you are a national of the UK, Republic of Ireland, US, Canada, Australia or New Zealand. Other travellers should consult the Belgian website (www.diplomatie.be), embassy or tourist office in their own country to find out about visa requirements.

Customs
Residents of the UK, Ireland and other EU countries may bring into Belgium personal possessions and goods for personal use, including a reasonable amount of tobacco and alcohol, provided they have been bought in the EU. There are few formalities at the point of entry into Belgium. Residents of non-EU countries, and EU residents arriving from a non-EU country, may bring in up to 400 cigarettes and 50 cigars or 50 g (2 oz) of tobacco, 2 litres (3 bottles) of wine and 1 litre (about 2 pints) of spirits and liqueurs.

MONEY
Cash
The euro (€) is the official currency in Belgium. €1 = 100 cents. It comes in notes of €5, €10, €20, €50, €100, €200 and €500. Coins are in denominations of €1 and €2, and 1, 2, 5, 10, 20 and 50 cents.

ATM machines can be found at the airport, railway stations, and in several locations around Bruges, including the main post office. They accept most British and international debit and credit cards.

They are the quickest and most convenient way (and often the cheapest) to obtain cash. Instructions are usually available in English and other major European languages.

De Post ⓐ Markt 5
Europabank ⓐ Vlamingstraat 13
Fortisbank ⓐ Simon Stevinplein 3
KBC ⓐ Steenstraat 38

Traveller's cheques

Traveller's cheques and foreign money can be cashed at most banks and bureaux de change. You may have to produce your passport or other ID. Traveller's cheques aren't widely accepted in restaurants and shops. Many hotels will also change money for you, but often at unfavourable rates. There are a number of exchange bureaux (Wissel) in Bruges:

Goffin Change ⓐ Steenstraat 2
Pillen R W J ⓐ Rozenhoedkaai 2
Tourist office ⓐ Concertgebouw, 't Zand 34

Credit cards

The most widely accepted credit cards are VISA and MasterCard, though other major credit cards, such as American Express, are also commonly accepted in restaurants and shops. At the time of writing, the chip-and-pin system, recently introduced in the UK, is not widely used in Belgium.

HEALTH, SAFETY & CRIME

The tap water in Bruges is safe, although many Belgians and visitors prefer to drink one of the many brands of mineral water. If you want tap water in a restaurant or café, you might find it difficult to get, because they would rather sell you bottled water.

Medical facilities in Belgium are of an excellent standard, but expensive – ensure you have adequate travel insurance. Most minor ailments can be taken to pharmacies (*apotheek*), indicated by a green cross sign. There are several in Bruges' city centre. Pharmacies have expert staff who are qualified to offer medical advice and dispense a wide range of medicines. Many drugs that are widely available in the UK are obtainable only at pharmacies in Belgium. Most hotels have lists of pharmacies, doctors and dentists. See 'Emergencies' page 156 for further details.

Bruges is a safe city, with little obvious crime but, as with every major tourist attraction, it draws its share of pickpockets, particularly in summer. You should remember to be vigilant at train stations. Otherwise, take normal, sensible precautions by being careful in crowds and avoiding deserted streets at night, although there will rarely be any danger.

You probably won't see much of Bruges' police (*politie*). There isn't a huge presence on the streets except during major events, but when they are around, they are friendly, efficient and helpful, and often speak English. (See 'Emergencies' for contact details.)

OPENING HOURS

Most shops are open 09.00–18.00 Mon–Sat. But many tourist and food shops are open on Sundays, and have longer hours. Some smaller shops close at lunchtime.

Bank opening hours vary: some normally open 09.30–12.00 & 14.00–16.00, others 09.00–12.30 & 13.30–16.15, although some branches are open during lunch, and others close earlier in the afternoon. All are open Mon–Fri, and closed on public holidays.

The main museums are open 09.30–17.00 Tues–Sun. Museums are closed on Mondays, except Easter and Whit Monday. Tickets are normally sold until 16.30 (16.15 at the Belfort). Opening times of churches vary.

The major markets (in Markt, 't Zand, Vismarkt and Beursplein) are open 08.00–13.00.

TOILETS

There are public toilets in the old market hall in the Belfort, in the Sint-Janshospitaal complex, at the railway station, in 't Zand Square and Bargplein, just south of Minnewaterpark. There is usually a small charge, but they are generally clean and well kept. Otherwise, all the main museums have good toilet facilities, as do the better bars, cafés and restaurants, and the leading hotels.

CHILDREN

Bruges is a pretty child-friendly place, and children are welcome in all but the most expensive restaurants (which they probably wouldn't enjoy anyway). Since there are no supermarkets in the city centre, it might be best to bring baby food, nappies, etc. with you. There are plenty of sweet shops and places selling chips, ice creams and waffles, so keeping tiny tummies happy shouldn't be too much of a challenge. But there are few attractions specifically geared to children. However, Astridpark has an adventure playground, and many children (particularly older ones) are likely to have a great time at Choco-Story (see page 92), the Archaeology Museum (see pages 74–5), the Folklore Museum (see pages 96–7), the windmills (see page 97), and taking a horse-drawn carriage or canal-boat ride. They might also find entertainment during the open-air events of some of Bruges' festivals (see pages 8–11).

Children under 13 are allowed free entrance to municipal museums (but not private ones).

COMMUNICATIONS

Phones

Public telephones (though there aren't that many around) accept a pre-paid phonecard, and sometimes coins. You can buy a phonecard from

---

TELEPHONING BELGIUM

To telephone Belgium from abroad, dial the international code first (usually 00), then 32, the area code minus the initial 0 (eg. 50 for Bruges), and the local number. When calling Belgium from within the country, you always need to dial the full area code, even if you are in the zone you are calling.

TELEPHONING FROM BELGIUM

To make an international call from Belgium, dial 00 first, then the country code, followed by the local area code (minus the initial 0 if there is one) and the local number.

Country codes:

Australia 61
Canada 1
New Zealand 64
Republic of Ireland 353
South Africa 27
UK 44
USA 1

International directory service 1304
National directory service 1405

the post office, railway stations and newsagents. Bruges is fine for mobile-phone coverage, though you will have to switch to a local network such as Proximus or Mobistar. Check with your service provider before you leave to find out which will be the cheapest for you.

Postal services

The Belgian postal service is generally efficient, and mail to the UK will normally take two or three days to arrive, a little longer to destinations outside Europe. You can buy stamps at the post office, newsagents and tobacconists. A standard letter or postcard to anywhere within Belgium is €0.46, to Europe €0.60, to the rest of the world €0.65. Bruges has several red postboxes, but also hole-in-the-wall postboxes. Look for the word Poste.

Main Post Office It is the only one in Bruges you are likely to use, and has an ATM. ➋ Markt 5, near the Belfort ◷ 09.00–17.00 Mon–Fri, 09.30–12.30 Sat, closed Sun

Internet

Bruges isn't particularly well served by internet cafés (though most of the bigger and more expensive hotels offer internet connections), but you can try out the following:

Bauhaus Cybercafé €1.30 for the first 15 minutes, then €0.08 per minute. ➋ Langestraat 145 ⓦ www.bauhaus.be

Snuffel Backpacker Hostel €1 per half hour. ➋ Ezelstraat 47–49 ☎ 050 33 31 33 ⓦ www.snuffel.be

Teleboetiek €1 an hour. ➋ corner of Langestraat & Predikherenstraat ☎ 050 61 67 69 ◷ 09.30–21.00 Mon–Sat, 10.30–21.00 Sun

The Coffee Link Within the Sint-Janshospitaal complex. €1.50 for the first 15 minutes, €5 for an hour. ⓐ Mariastraat 38 ❶ 050 34 99 73 ⓦ www.thecoffeelink.com 🕐 10.00–18.00 Tues–Sat, 12.00–18.00 Mon, closed Sun

ELECTRICITY

Belgium runs on 220 volts with two-pin plugs. British appliances will need a simple adaptor, best obtained in most UK electrical shops, or at the Eurostar station or airport. You will also be able to find shops in Bruges selling adaptors, but you might have difficulty finding one in the centre. US and other equipment designed for 110 volts will need a transformer.

TRAVELLERS WITH DISABILITIES

Although a number of the museums, restaurants and hotels have access facilities usable by visitors with mobility problems, it must be said that Bruges, with its cobbled streets, medieval buildings, pedestrianised areas, large number of tourists and limited flow for motor vehicles, isn't the ideal destination for disabled visitors. Nor are trains, buses or most taxis adapted to the needs of disabled visitors, although much progress has been made in Bruges in recent years. You can get advice from the Bruges tourist office (see page 152) and on www.accessiblebruges.be, which uses pictograms to illustrate the facilities available in a number of buildings. Other useful organisations for advice and information include:

RADAR The principal UK forum and pressure group for people with disabilities. ⓐ 12 City Forum, 250 City Road, London EC1V 8AF ❶ 0207 250 3222 ⓦ www.radar.org.uk

SATH (Society for Accessible Travel & Hospitality) Advises US-based travellers with disabilities. ⓐ 347 Fifth Ave, Suite 610, New York, NY 10016 ⓣ 212 447 7284 ⓦ www.sath.org

FURTHER INFORMATION

There are two tourist information offices in Bruges, one at the railway station, and one (In&Uit Brugge) at the Concertgebouw, which also sells tickets.

In&Uit Brugge You can get a map, a guide to the city's attractions (both for a small charge), an events listing and various books. You can also get internet access and book hotel rooms there. ⓐ Concertgebouw, 't Zand 34 ⓣ 050 44 86 86 ⓛ 10.00–18.00 Fri–Wed, 10.00–20.00 Thur

Railway Station ⓛ 09.30–12.30 & 13.00–17.00 Tues–Sat

Useful websites include:
www.brugge.be. The tourist office website for the city. There are listings of accommodation, municipal museums and events.
www.tinck.be. Online and telephone (070 22 50 05) information and ticket booking for cultural events.
www.visitbelgium.com. The official Belgian tourist website.
www.visitflanders.co.uk. The official Flanders website.

▶ *Enjoying the sun by the statue of Jan Breydel Maertens*

Useful phrases

Although English is widely spoken in Bruges, these Dutch words and phrases may come in handy. See also the phrases for specific situations in other parts of the book.

English	Dutch	Approx. pronunciation
BASICS		
Yes	Ja	Ya
No	Nee	Nay
Please (requesting)	Alstublieft	Als-too-bleeft
Thank you	Dank u wel	Dank oo vel
Hello	Dag/hallo	Dakh/hallo
Goodbye	Dag/tot ziens	Dakh/tot zeens
Excuse me	Pardon	Par-don
Sorry	Sorry	Soree
That's all right	Dat geeft niet, hoor	Dat khayft neet, hor
I don't speak any	Ik spreek geen	Ik sprayk khayn
Do you speak English?	Spreekt u Engels?	Spraykt-oo Eng-els?
Good morning	Goedemorgen	Khooda-morkha
Good afternoon	Goedemiddag	Khooda-middakh
Good evening	Goedenavond	Khoodan-afont
Goodnight	Goedenacht	Khooda-nakht
My name's ...	Ik heet ...	Ik hayt ...

English	Dutch	Approx. pronunciation
DAYS & TIMES		
Monday	Maandag	Maan-dakh
Tuesday	Dinsdag	Dins-dakh
Wednesday	Woensdag	Woons-dakh
Thursday	Donderdag	Donder-dakh
Friday	Vrijdag	Fraye-dakh
Saturday	Zaterdag	Zater-dakh
Sunday	Zondag	Zon-dakh
Morning	Morgens	Morkhens
Afternoon	Middags	middakhs
Evening	Avonds	Afonds
Night	Nachts	Nakhts
Yesterday	Gisteren	Khistera
Today	Vandaag	Fan-dakh
Tomorrow	Morgen	Morkhen

English	Dutch	Approx. pronunciation
What time?	Om hoe laat?	Om hoo laat?
It's nine o'clock (am)	Het is negen uur	Het is naykhen oor
Twelve noon	Het is twaalf uur 's middags	Het is twal-ef oor smiddakhs
Midnight	Het is twaalf uur 's nachts	Het is twal-ef oor snakhts

NUMBERS

One	Een	Ayn
Two	Twee	Tway
Three	Drie	Dree
Four	Vier	Feer
Five	Vijf	Fayef
Six	Zes	Zess
Seven	Zeven	Zayfen
Eight	Acht	Akht
Nine	Negen	Naykhen
Ten	Tien	Teen
Eleven	Elf	El-ef
Twelve	Twaalf	Twaal-ef
Twenty	Twintig	Twintikh
Fifty	Vijftig	Fayeftikh
One hundred	Honderd	Honderd

MONEY

Where can I find a bank around here?	Waar is hier ergens een bank?	Vaar is hier er-khens an bank?
I'd like to change some money	Ik wil graag geld wisselen	Ik vil khraakh khelt vissela
Do you take credit cards?	Kan ik met een creditcard betalen?	Kan ik met an creditcart betalen?

SIGNS & NOTICES

Airport	Vliegveld	Fleekh-felt
Station	Station	Sta-syon
Platform	Spoor/perron	Spoar/perron
Smoking compartment	Rookcoupé	Roak-koopay
Toilet	WC	Way say
Underground	Metro	May-troh

Emergencies

MEDICAL SERVICES
Emergency numbers
Emergency medical services 100
Fire brigade 100
Doctors (information on nearest on-duty) 100
Doctors on weekend call 050 36 40 10 (20.00 Fri–08.00 Mon)
Pharmacists on weekend call 050 40 61 62 or 0900 10 500
(09.00–22.00), 101 (22.00–09.00)
Dentists (information on nearest on-duty) 100

Hospitals & clinics
AZ St Jan ⓐ Ruddershove 10 ⓣ 050 45 21 11, emergencies 050 45 20 00
St Franciscus Xaveriuskliniek ⓐ Spaanse Loskaai 1 ⓣ 050 47 04 70
St Lucas ⓐ St Lucaslaan 29 ⓣ 050 36 91 11

EMERGENCY PHRASES

Help!
Hulp!
Hul-ep!

Call the police!
Bel de politie!
Bel de pol-eet-see!

Fire!
Brand!
Brant!

Call the fire brigade!
Bel de brandweer!
Bel de brant-veer!

Stop!
Stop!
stop!

Call an ambulance!
Bel een ziekenauto!
Bel an zeeken-owtoe!

POLICE
Central Station ◎ Hauwerstraat 7 ❶ 050 44 89 30

EMBASSIES
Australia ◎ Guimard Centre, Rue Guimard 6–8, Brussels ❶ 02 286 05 00
Canada ◎ Avenue de Tervueren 2, Brussels ❶ 02 741 06 11
New Zealand ◎ Square de Meeûs, 7th floor, Brussels ❶ 02 512 10 40
Republic of Ireland ◎ Rue Wiertz (Wierstraat) 50, Brussels ❶ 02 230 53 37
South Africa ◎ Rue de la Loi b-7/8, Brussels ❶ 02 285 44 00
UK ◎ Rue Arlon (Aarlenstraat) 85, Brussels ❶ 02 287 62 11
USA Boulevard de Régent (Regentlaan) 27, Brussels ❶ 02 508 21 11

⬤ *The lake in Bruges' Minnewaterpark*

A

accommodation 34–39, 127–128, 140
Adoration of the Mystic Lamb (van Eyck & van Eyck) 121–122
air travel 142
airports 48–49, 142
Archaeology Museum 74, 76
architecture 44–45, 116
Arentshuis 76
Arentspark 76
arts see culture
ATMs 145–146

B

bars, clubs & pubs 30–31, 73, 88–89, 127, 139
battlefield visits 132–133, 135
bed & breakfast 38
beer 28, 79
Begijnhof 76–78
Belfort (Bruges) 60, 63
Belfort (Ghent) 118–119
bookselling 110
Brangwyn Museum 76
bureaux de change 146
Burg 60, 63
bus travel 48, 49–50, 106

C

cafés 60, 68–69, 85, 86, 125, 139, 150–151
canal tours 58, 90, 106, 116
car hire 58
children 148–149
chocolate 24, 83, 85, 92
Choco-Story 92
cinema 20, 31
Cloth Hall 135
coach travel 51, 132
Concertgebouw 20, 78
credit cards 146

crime 54, 147
culture 18–20, 31, 46, 60, 63–66, 74, 76–83, 92–97, 108–110, 116–117, 118–122, 136
customs and duty 145
cycling 32, 58, 106, 132

D

Damme 104–108
De Halve Maan Brewery 79
Design Museum 120
Diamant Museum 79
diamonds 79
disabilities, travellers with 151–152
driving 51, 54, 132, 144

E

electricity 151
embassies 157
emergencies 156–157
Engels Klooster 93–94
entertainment 10, 20, 30–31 see also nightlife
events 8–13, 20, 31, 116–117
Eyck, Jan & Hubert van 121–122

F

ferry travel 144–145
festivals 9, 10, 11, 12–13, 20, 31, 116–117
food & drink 24–25, 26–29, 46, 66, 67, 79, 83, 85, 92, 123, 125, 146–147
football 32

G

Geldmuntstraat 66
Gezelle, Guido 94
Ghent 114–118
Ghent Festivities 116–117
gin 28
golf 32–33

Gravensteen 120
Groeninge Museum 79–80
Grote Markt 135
Gruuthuse Museum 81
Guido Gezelle Museum 94

H

health 146–147, 156
Heiligbloed Basiliek 64
history 14–15, 104, 130
hotels 34–38, 127–128, 140

I

In Flanders Fields Museum 136
insurance 144
internet cafés 150–151

J

Jan van Eyckplein 92
Jeruzalemkerk 94–95

K

Kantcentrum 95
Kasselrij 135
Kruisvest 97

L

lace 24, 66, 95
languages 16, 25, 29, 54, 154–155, 156
lifestyle 16–17, 54

M

markets 25, 83, 123
Markt 60, 62
Memling Museum 82
Menin Gate 136
money 145–146
Museum voor Schone Kunsten (MSK) 120–121
Museum voor Volkskunde 96–97
music 10, 20, 31, 73

N

Nieuwerck 135

nightlife 10, 20, 30–31, 70, 72–73, 87–89, 101–102, 112–113, 125–127, 139–140
Noordzandstraat 83
Northeast of Markt 90–92

O
Onze-Lieve-Vrouw ter Potterie 95
Onze-Lieve-Vrouwekerk (Bruges) 81–82
Onze-Lieve-Vrouwekerk (Damme) 108
opening hours 11, 26–27, 30–31, 147–148

P
Paleis van het Brugse Vrije 64
passports & visas 145
phones 149–150
police 147
post 150
Procession of the Holy Blood 12–13
Provinciaal Hof 60, 62
public holidays 11
public transport 48, 49–51, 106, 114, 132, 142–144

R
rail travel 48, 49, 50–51, 114, 132, 142–144
restaurants 26–28, 70, 72–73, 85, 86, 87–88, 101–102, 112–113, 125–127, 139–140

S
safety 26, 54–55, 146–147
St Anna 90, 92
Schellemolen 108
seasons 8
shopping 22–25, 66–67, 83, 85, 97–99, 110, 122–123, 125
Sint-Annakerk 95–96
Sint-Baafskathedraal 121–122
Sint-Janshospitaal (Bruges) 82–83
Sint-Janshospitaal (Damme) 108–109
Sint-Walburgakerk 96
South of Markt 74
sport 32–33
Stadhuis (Bruges) 66
Stadhuis (Damme) 109–110
Stedelijk Museum voor Actuele Kunst (SMAK) 122

Steenstraat 66
swimming 33

T
taxis 48, 49–50, 58, 114
tea rooms 85, 86
Ter Beurze house 90
time differences 48
tipping 26
toilets 148
tourist information 152
Toyo Ito Pavilion 63
tram travel 114
traveller's cheques 146

W
walking 33, 44–45, 58
water 26, 146–147
weather 8, 46
windmills 97, 108
windmills of the Kruisvest 97
Wollestraat 66

Y
youth hostels 38–39
Ypres 130–136

Z
Zilverpand 83
Zuidzandstraat 83

The publishers would like to thank the following for supplying the copyright photographs for this book:
Tourism Flanders pages: 1, 5, 7, 13, 24, 49, 50, 55, 62, 77, 89, 98, 112, 133, 153, 157; all the rest Anwer Bati.

Copy editor: Anne McGregor
Proofreader: Penny Isaac

Send your thoughts to
books@thomascook.com

- Found a great bar, club, shop or must-see sight that we don't feature?

- Like to tip us off about any information that needs updating?

- Want to tell us what you love about this handy little guidebook and more importantly how we can make it even handier?

Then here's your chance to tell all! Send us ideas, discoveries and recommendations today and then look out for your valuable input in the next edition of this title. As an extra 'thank you' from Thomas Cook Publishing, you'll be automatically entered into our exciting monthly prize draw.

Send an email to the above address (stating the book's title) or write to: CitySpots Project Editor, Thomas Cook Publishing, PO Box 227, The Thomas Cook Business Park, Unit 18, Coningsby Road, Peterborough PE3 8SB, UK.